WHY WILL NO-ONE PUBLISH MY NOVEL?

After hard times and odd jobs as a lone parent FAY WELDON became one of the top advertising copywriters of her generation. She moved to TV drama (writing the pilot episode of the iconic series *Upstairs Downstairs*) then turned to novels – including the classic *The Life and Loves of a She Devil* and *The Cloning of Joanna May*. A sequel to her acclaimed Love and Inheritance trilogy, *Before the War*, was published in 2017. Fay's been made a CBE for services to literature and she's currently a Professor of Creative Writing at Bath Spa University.

ALSO BY FAY WELDON

FICTION

The Fat Woman's Joke
Down Among the Women
Female Friends
Remember Me
Little Sisters
Praxis
Puffball
The President's Child
The Life and Loves of a She Devil
The Shrapnel Academy
The Heart of the Country
The Hearts and Lives of Men
The Rules of Life
Leader of the Band
The Cloning of Joanna May
Darcy's Utopia
Growing Rich
Life Force
Affliction
Splitting
Worst Fears
Big Women
Rhode Island Blues
The Bulgari Connection
Mantrapped
She May Not Leave
The Spa Decamaron
The Stepmother's Diary
Chalcot Crescent
Kehua!

Habits of the House
Long Live the King
The New Countess
The Ted Dreams
Before The War
Death of a She Devil

CHILDREN'S BOOKS

Wolf the Mechanical Dog
Party Puddle
Nobody Likes Me

SHORT STORY COLLECTIONS

Watching Me, Watching You
Polaris
Moon Over Minneapolis
Wicked Women
A Hard Time to Be a Father
Nothing to Wear & Nowhere to Hide
Mischief

NON-FICTION

Letters to Alice
Rebecca West
Sacred Cows
Godless in Eden
Auto da Fay
What Makes Women Happy

WHY WILL NO-ONE PUBLISH MY NOVEL?

A Handbook For
The Rejected Writer

Fay Weldon

First published in the UK in 2018 by Head of Zeus Ltd

9 7 5 3 1 2 4 6 8

A catalogue record for this book is available from
the British Library.

ISBN (HB): 9781788544610
ISBN (E): 9781788544603

Printed and bound in Germany by CPI Books GmbH

Head of Zeus Ltd
First Floor East
5–8 Hardwick Street
London EC1R 4RG

WWW.HEADOFZEUS.COM

Contents

Part One

Poor you…   3

Why they said no   5

Part Two

No-one knows anything, but trust

is important   47

Six rejections? It really is too bad!   50

First of all, know your enemy   55

Find out the basics – what exactly

is a literary agency?   57

But what happens if you're a man in
this feminised world?   67

Part Three
How to keep the reader happy   71
The rules and non-rules of writing   73

Part Four
Frequently asked questions –
a revision guide   115

Part Five
A life in writing   169

Finale   184
Further reading   186

Part One

Poor you…

Let's get the *poor me*'s over with. Self-pity does not become you. You will develop a wrinkled brow and a turned-down mouth.

All the same, it is a blow, as Mr Rochester, staggering, said to Jane Eyre when Mr Mason turned up unexpectedly from the West Indies. 'Jane, I've got a blow; I've got a blow, Jane!'

'Sorry, not for us' – *not for us, not for us, not for us, not for us, not for us* – rejected six times… Ouch!

All that time wasted, all that endeavour, all that

wrestling with language, tenses, structure, all that time taken away from family and friends, and for what? For nothing.

Bitter. A humiliation. A blow. A public failure.

Okay. Over. But what next? Six times means re-think time.

Don't panic. Just ask yourself why. Work out what went wrong. Why no-one wants the novel on which you worked so hard. Research says that 80 per cent of all submitted manuscripts are rejected, and I have no reason to doubt it. But ask yourself exactly what category (or categories) yours may have fallen into – what pigeonhole.

Face it. Be brave. Check the possibilities described below. Then *do* something about it. Look, learn, re-draft. Edit. Re-edit. Send nothing out that you do not believe to be perfect, that you can't argue for word by word. Well, within limits. And best to know these limits. Read on.

Why they said no

Which pigeonhole was yours?

a) Perhaps your novel was just plain boring?

b) Perhaps you had nothing to say.

c) Perhaps it had no structure: came to no conclusion: wandered all over the place.

d) Perhaps it was too old-fashioned: you're out of touch with the new world.

e) Perhaps there's no USP – unique selling proposition – and though editors loved it, Marketing didn't think they could sell it. (These days Marketing rules the roost.)

f) Perhaps it was likely to upset too many people. Controversial.

g) Perhaps your synopsis failed to explain your novel as well as it could.

h) Perhaps it's too good for them – too much fine writing, too little plot.

i) Perhaps they didn't get further than page one before rejecting you as illiterate, not sufficiently educated.

Anyway, your novel's been rejected six times, and no-one's told you why. Let's take these possibilities one at a time. Be brave. Do not be defeated. Learn from them. More than one pigeonhole may apply, and all too often does.

a) Too boring

Don't take this as an insult. It doesn't mean you are a boring person – no-one who undertakes and has the stamina and will to complete a whole novel is boring, believe me – just that you may well have failed to put into the novel the spark that makes you what you are, and why you chose to write it in the first place, and it shows.

Your novel is dull. It has been written with great care, but perhaps using the left side of the brain, the rational, sensible, censorious, red-pencil side, leaving the woozy, fuzzy, dreamy, inventive, right side out altogether.

You may well have used one of the many *How to Write a Novel* instruction manuals around, and followed all the rules, but it's wooden, static, lacks any sense of imperative, of a story that has to be written and demands to be read. Whatever its genre, comedy or tragedy, romance or dystopia, light-hearted or grim, who cares? You wanted to stay anonymous, shelter behind the mechanics of your plot, divorce yourself from your characters – ignoring the fact that they must be some aspect of yourself or how could, why would, you have made them up in the first place?

You refused to lose your good opinion of yourself. Your leading character steals, lies, fornicates, cheats – 'nothing to do with me', you told the world. Foolish! Hiding was a mistake. One that will take a lot of rectifying, but it can be done. Though it'll need courage.

A writer needs a fair bit of introspection to succeed. I spent five years in psychoanalysis before I was sane enough to write anything longer or more interesting than an advertisement, poor craven wretch of a copywriter that I was, though with a nifty turn of phrase, but little else until then. I could sell product pretty well, but not ideas: I exhausted myself after a couple of paragraphs and craved immediate results. In advertising it's *write today, in the paper tomorrow*. All short-term stuff. In novel writing you're in for the long haul. Take yourself seriously. Know who you are, what you are, and why you are writing. It's the hiding from the self that makes one boring on the page. So forget any delusion that you're a nice person, you're as awful and evil as the worst person you ever imagined. This stuff has to come from somewhere. Abandon your good opinion of yourself before you start your rewrite.

Many fiction writers, it seems to me, are working out on the page the painful problems of their childhood and family, however disguised this is from themselves and others. Some can get it over with in their first novel and lose the desire to write thereafter; they're the lucky ones. Some go on puzzling and niggling and suffering for the rest of their lives, as I did. (Well, not exactly suffering – those were the angry, funny, feminist novels of my youth, which mixed rage with levity, and spoke for an indignant generation.) But I still obsess as to why my puritanical mother was like she was and my darling absent father the way he was, and never paid maintenance. The war between the sexes. I've never got over it.

It's not just novelists, either. See it in historians. Consider the case of Edward Gibbon, celebrated eighteenth-century historian and belle-lettrist, much of whose life was spent writing the magnificent and entertaining (for those days) six-volume *History of the Decline and Fall of the Roman Empire*, proving that the fall of Rome was the result of the dawn of Christianity. He described himself as 'a puny child, neglected by my Mother, starved by my nurse'. He had five siblings, all of whom died in infancy, but still, he complained, his very Christian mother 'treated him with disdain'. As the Duke of Gloucester remarked to him in 1781: 'Another damned, thick, square book! Always scribble, scribble, scribble! Eh! Mr Gibbon?'

Well, of course. Never got over it. Still puzzling and niggling away at the past, his own or the world's. What's the difference? To the child, the home is the world.

Of course a novel shouldn't be over-autobiographical – but needs to be written by a human, not a reporting robot, rule obsessed. It's an act of communication between writer and reader. If you try and hide yourself too much (your personality as echoed in the enthusiasms, pains and rages of your characters – all hidden aspects of you, remember) and just report what these characters do, readers will shut off because you have failed to engage them.

It's been a 'not for us' six times over, though no agent or publisher will tell you why to your face. Boring! Though they won't say this – it sounds too crude and unkind.

If you suspect that 'boring' is the main reason, but the desire to write remains stubborn, and you are not open to self-inspection, then perhaps do just start afresh, taking care to also avoid the traps listed in (b) to (i).

b) Nothing to say

Another major complaint from the agents about the state of the contemporary novel is that so often it has 'nothing to say': all plot, no purpose, no different from any of the others that come pouring in. There's no proper problem and so no possible resolution. It (your novel) just seems to go wandering and wondering on.

'Nothing much against this particular novel,' says the agent, 'just nothing much going for it, at least that Marketing will understand. I mean, *why?*' Yawn, yawn.

(And from the sound of it you wouldn't be much fun for the agent, let alone the publisher, when it came to taking you out to lunch. This does count. They're only human. And 'meeting writers' is one of the reasons they give for taking the job in the first place. So do make yourself agreeable: someone worth meeting. A little eccentricity never goes amiss.)

And so your novel went into the reject pile. In the old days such piles of yellowing paper, often handwritten and tear-stained (to prove just how desperate the writer was), were so high and all over the place you could hardly get into the publisher's office without tripping. These days rejects are just neatly packed away into a computer file for the intern to deal with and send out the 'not for us's. The offices are all steel and glass, and not old oak beams. Oh, and publishers' offices used to smell so romantically of polished mahogany, warm paper glue and printing ink. No longer. But enough of this nostalgia.

Publishing is an industry and not a 'gentleman's profession' any more. Today's novels, thanks probably to the blossoming of the creative writing class, are written to a far higher standard than they used to be. Look at a short story in any woman's magazine circa 1960 and shrink back in horror. No-one expected them to have 'something to say'. Those tear-stained paper piles contained far more rubbish than you'll find in any equivalent computer files today. Courage! Onward and upward!

It's always a bit vague – this cause for rejection, this 'nothing to say' business – and like 'boring', seldom spoken aloud to the client, let alone written. Too damning and disheartening, even more so than the 'boring' accusation. Of course you have something to say (80,000 words or so), but you didn't formulate it clearly enough to yourself, let alone to a reader, when you began. You didn't stay on track because you weren't sure what your track was. It'll be in there somewhere but it just needs finding. Be brave, and find it. Boil your whole novel down to one sentence – what I call your Cosmic Statement

WHY THEY SAID NO

– then go for it. Look at it like this. A novel is about more than its plot. Plots are easy. They can be changed at the click or so of the mouse. The girl who's carried out to sea by a rogue wave and you intend to drown can be carried back by another wave and live, washed up stranded on the seashore in her see-through swimsuit for the hero to admire. Plot is your servant, not the other way round. Your characters are there to make the plot plausible. Events are there to make the plot work.

So look for what you were trying to say in the first place. It's in there somewhere, the good idea that launched the whole process; the loving phrase spoken, the hateful comment made, the telling conversation overheard, the news item read – whatever it was that impelled you to take up your pen or keyboard.

Any novel flows more easily towards an inevitable conclusion if the writer writes with their Cosmic Statement – call it the 'mission statement' if you will

– in mind. Don't let it fall by the way. This 'something to say', the hypothesis, the underpinning, of what you're setting out to demonstrate. It can be simple, as in a romantic novel – *true love always finds a way* – to keep you on track, as the lover knocks down one obstacle after another on his journey towards the orgasm, the QED, the *quod erat demonstrandum* of the science lab. The writer provided characters and events to prove what had to be proved, and gets to the QED after a straight run through.

Sometimes a novelist gets their mission statement into their first line (very clever) and tells the world. '*It is a truth universally acknowledged, that a single man in possession of a good fortune, must be in want of a wife*' (Jane Austen), or '*It was the best of times, it was the worst of times*' (Charles Dickens), or '*The past is a foreign country. They do things differently there*' (L.P. Hartley).

Sometimes you only discover it when you're a third of the way through your novel, and have to go back and do a lot of re-writing. Having discovered it, stick to the point. Don't be so in love with your own writing that you go wandering off and lose sight of your initial story. You can only deal properly with one human problem at a time in your novel. One novel, one mission statement. Don't try to save the world in one go. With any luck you have a lifetime of novels waiting to be written ahead of you – there's so much in life to be said – so spread your material thin. It's precious.

And then no mere agent, no mere publisher, can say you have nothing to say.

c) Structure

Your novel had no structure, wandered around all over the place, came to no obvious conclusion?

Structure is not easy. 'Lack of structure' is the most frequent comment made by the rejecting authorities, and 'I can't *DO* structure' is the most frequent complaint I've come across, usually, alas, from the most talented and lyrical of writers. They're so in love with their own writing they forget there's anything else to worry about. Such as the plot.

But there is a really simple way of producing a structurally fail-safe novel which I will pass on to you, though it feels rather like cheating.

Try approaching your novel as you would a scientific experiment: the kind you did in the school chemistry lab. To get to the QED of a novel, the 'which was to be proved', all you need is a hypothesis, some ingredients, a set of methods and the QED is all yours. You may still be accused of (a) boring, and anything up to (g), but (c) will never get you.

Forming your hypothesis is the only difficult part in something that looks so easy. It's the cosmic sentence, the mission statement I've been talking about in (b). It's the sentence that sums up the thought that started you off, the idea that caught you all of a sudden, the emotion you were trying to validate, the point you were trying to prove. It's what your novel is 'about': why you wanted to write it in the first place (often rather vague and fuzzy and right-brainy), boiled down to just a couple of lines; one, even. It's what you wanted 'to say'.

Your hypothesis (defined as a 'proposed supposition for the purpose of investigation') will go something like this:

+ Dickens' *Tale of two Cities*: Good can come out of bad, the same as bad out of good.
+ Flynn's *Gone Girl*: We all lie about our perfect marriages – the better a marriage looks on the surface, the worse the secrets it holds!
+ Weldon's *Stepmother's Diary*: We all know stepmothers are wicked – but what about stepdaughters? They can be a whole lot worse!

I am including this last not out of vanity, but because once it was written and I was talking about it at some festival, I realised *The Stepmother's Diary* followed all my rules for a classic lab-created novel. More, it had been surprisingly easy to write: I'd known exactly what I was doing and so where I was going.

I wrote the novel after listening to a group of Danish stepmothers bewailing the sheer cruelty of their stepdaughters: how the second or third or even fourth (this was, after all, Scandinavia) marriages had not survived because of the machinations of the stepdaughters. It seemed to me to apply in the UK too – anywhere blended families are plentiful, and in the West that's nearly everywhere.

Thus:

1. **Hypothesis:** We all know stepmothers are wicked – but what about stepdaughters? They can be a whole lot worse!

2. **Ingredients:** A computer, a printer, a brain, access to your unconscious (more of which later).

3. **Method:**

   a) Choose characters that are going to prove your point and not wander off on their own. In this case a stepdaughter, a father, a stepmother, a grandmother as credible witness, being a Freudian analyst having an affair with her Jungian lodger. Don't be seduced by some fascinating character you once met in real life; he or she is useless to you – start them off as suitable stereotypes and bring them to life little by little through the novel as you discover their idiosyncrasies. They'll end up 'rounded' enough.

   b) Choose events that are going to demonstrate the truth of your hypothesis – in this case by the stepdaughter turning her father against the new wife, undermining the stepmother's self-esteem, ensuring her public disgrace, spending all father's credit cards up to the hilt, making sure stepmother's struggles to prove otherwise are to no avail, inspiring stepdaughter's friends to behave likewise and so on.

c) Stir all ingredients together, working all inexorably towards an inevitable end (chronological order's usually best – not too much back story).

4. **Result:** Loving marriage collapses as a result of interference from stepchild. A child is forever. A spouse is only temporary.

5. **Conclusion:** Stepmothers can be wicked – but what about stepdaughters? They're a whole lot worse!

6. **QED:** Which was to be proved.

Now there is a structure. Everyone is satisfied. Writer, reader, publisher. Your story feels like the truth, though everything has been invented – just carried to extremes.

d) Perhaps it was too old-fashioned, too previous century

The writer is writing the same old thing, complains Marketing: he or she hasn't seemed to notice that society is moving on, changing; is vegan as well as carnivore. That women are no longer the passive, uncritical creatures they used to be, who ask men questions because men know best and then wait for the answers. Feisty is in, dependent is out.

It's not so much that characters have changed since you were a child but writing styles have as well. Since the advent of the computer, sentences are shorter, verbs are quieter, adjectives and adverbs, especially the latter, are used sparsely, and with more elaboration; today's agents and publishers like informative detail, not just the writer telling the reader what characters do, but understanding how and why they do it.

Thus a simple 'he grinned' is out. (Sloppy. There

are so many different ways of grinning – be more precise.) 'He smiled a mirthless/joyous/bitter grin' is in.

'She sipped her wine' is out. (Boring, not needed: 'sipping wine' like 'drinking tea' just holds the action up – unless it is the action, and the reader already knows that the wine or tea is poisoned and the sipping will result in death.) 'Delete or expand' is the golden rule. If the scene survives perfectly without a particular word, do without it. If it's important or interesting, tell us more. Try instead 'She sipped her 1998 Dom Perignon and marvelled at his wealth / revelled in its expensive bubbles / found it too acid on her palate'. This would be worth saying, so say it.

'"I hate you", she yelled' is out. (Yes, but how exactly did she yell? And surely heroines, however provoked, never do yell? It's so unattractive.) Try 'The words "I hate you!" burst from her battered lips, summing up years of pent-up fury', or some such. Heroines can hate, but not yell. Odd, but there it is.

Hand-me-down verbs (like grinned, sipped, yelled, chuckled) just on their own are best suited to screenplays as brief instructions to an actor, too crude for the written page, where they need qualification.

The accusation 'old-fashioned' is difficult to refute, since it is often the sign of a writer who hasn't read a novel since childhood and 'doesn't keep up'.

The same goes for present participles (often called hanging participles) – crossing rooms, sitting down, standing up, walking towards – if you find yourself using them to start a sentence, just don't.

'*Looking to the East, the sun was rising,*' or '*Crossing the road, she said hello to John.*' Ouch! It's so easy to go wrong when describing simultaneous actions – they so seldom are. '*She looked to the East and saw that the sun was rising*' or '*She crossed the road and said hello to John'* is what you mean, and feels younger and more immediate, less out of an older literary tradition. The contemporary novel favours keeping things clear and simple and abhors the participle form of the verb even when it is used correctly. And then, and then, and then: one thing at a time, please, and keep it short, avoid those complicated and confusing sentences.

Or perhaps you've noticeably avoided the lovely little neutral word 'said', as you were told to by some old-fashioned writing teacher in the past. So instead of just 'saying' in a section of dialogue so we know who's speaking, your characters will opine, argue, refute, expostulate, apologise, interrupt, squeal, snort, beg, chatter, amend, enthuse, gush, moan, comment, allude, criticise, appreciate and so on – anything, anything to avoid the word 'said' – to such a degree your sophisticated reader jeers. If you need to explain how someone says something by all means do so, but don't try to do it by elaborating on 'said'. It's a word so simple and innocent no-one even notices it in reading-and-noting tests, other than by its absence, as readers puzzle over who's saying what to whom, and get annoyed. Be more interested in the reader's reaction than in your own ingenuity.

The contemporary writer uses the word 'said', and then, if it's important, and having taken time (well, a second or two) to think about it, tells the reader exactly how it was said.

'"Oh, well done!" Marlene said. Her enthusiasm was intoxicating.'

And talking of exclamation marks, the 'screamers' of old-fashioned yellow-press journalism: do too many of them spoil the clean crisp appearance of your text on the screen? Look inside any Angela Brazil (1868–1947) book on Amazon to see what I mean by old-fashioned. In ten lines of dialogue twelve exclamation marks. Mind you, that was the 'young adult book' of her time and you could tell a young girl by her breathlessness. But Brazil didn't half sell – a great strong verb advocate: she too living in apparent fear of 'said'. In *The Nicest Girl in the School* (1909), she manages twenty-eight lines of verbal exchanges with not a single 'she said', but instead a yelled, suggested, volunteered, listened, sighed, puzzled, continued, marvelled, complained, shouted and corrected, all accompanied by an exclamation mark at the end of a sentence.

Do be prudent with your adjectives: use them sparingly, realising that every one you use deprives the next one of power. '*Sara's lovely, lustrous, chestnut hair tumbled longingly round her perfect heart-shaped face, reaching down tenderly in riotous curls to meet the enchanting curve of her pale, tip-tilted bosom*' is not likely to warm the cockles of today's cold and critical agent heart, no matter how proud of it you may be. (Suspiciously male-egocentric anyway.) Adjectival and adverbial clauses should take their place, saying the same thing but taking longer. More detailed.

A simile might come in handy, or a metaphor. And forget the name Sara – a staple girlfriend's name in the old dick-lit – try Syrah instead. *'Syrah's red hair, glossy as an over-ripe chestnut, fell to the sculptural perfection of her naked breasts.'*

Anyway, go through your manuscript to check any surplus of adjectives and adverbs, stray participle phrases, too few 'saids', and old-school names, only then re-submit. If to an agent you've tried before then perhaps change the title, the name and the synopsis just in case it's the same intern who gets it.

And if you're over fifty, do remember that so many of your readers are going to be Millennials, leaping and bounding, preferring not to see or think about anyone who lives in sight or thought of their own mortality. I don't blame them. Just try not to teach them better. Be a little less sententious when dealing with them as characters. If sentimentality replaces sentiment, if 'now' is all that matters, if they ignore the past in order not to fear the future, if they believe they have arrived at the perfect present, well, let them. They'll learn, poor things. Don't let it show that you favour the old against the young: there is quite a battle going on.

I really want you to get your book published. I want you to make sense of your own self-created universe. For me it's almost a sacred mission: I'm a born proselytiser. As the evangelist hopes others will be saved and go to heaven, or sink back into the darkness of hell, so I hope others will hear and get published, not sink back into the outer darkness of rejection.

e) There's no USP – unique selling proposition

Your novel has got through the first barriers, been accepted by a literary agency, and is now coming up on the screens of the acquisitions team of a big publisher. Oh, well done you!

Let's call it *Whence Aramintha?* for the sake of argument.

'Terrible title, but it's a literary novel – and so beautifully written.' Blanche, newly promoted Commissioning Editor, is doing the pitching. She really likes *Aramintha* and has rung up the agency to say so. But now 'First Novels, New Authors' has come up on the agenda she's nervous. She knows *Aramintha* will be a hard sell and the author won't change the title. *Literary Novels Under Threat*, shrieks this week's *Bookseller*, the publishing trade journal. Sales are atrocious. Genre novels are doing just fine – well, fine-ish, reading the small print. 'I know nothing much happens but it's magical,' Blanche goes on.

'Worse and worse,' grumbles Jared from Marketing. 'Nothing happens! Where's it set – Hampstead?'

'A bit further out of London, as it happens, but does that matter? The writer has a real gift for words.

31

It's like a *Wide Sargasso Sea* but set in a suburb. Such a gift with metaphor it thrills. One really feels for the characters and their quandary.' Blanche is doing her best with the material she's got.

'What's their quandary?'

'Well, it *is* a bit vague.' Blanche hasn't had much help from your synopsis and the agent didn't get round to tidying it up. 'Four characters trapped in their marriages, trying to arrive at a definition of love.'

'Don't tell me. Set in a nameless outer suburb in North London with characters called Crispin and Jasper, Aramintha and Adelaide (or Addie for short), and the "nothing much" that happens is a long argument about recycling the vegetables. It's a burgeoning field. Are they vegans?'

Blanche nods, numbly.

'Flash in the pan. We had three like it published last year, everything white, white, middle, middle, and politically correct. All of them vegan. Writers love them, readers hate them. None of them sold. No-one gets married any more anyway. For pity's sake, Blanche, give me something I can sell!' And Blanche shrinks back into her literary shell and it's a 'no, not for us', and back to the agent. Blanche is young and new to the game; she didn't prepare her defences properly, and you were too fancy a writer to have provided useful statistics about novel-reading vegans which might have helped Blanche.

What Jared craves is something which will make a splash in the *Mail* (historical abuse is always a winner), or the *Guardian* (anything set in Afghanistan or the Yemen, but the Bardo Thodol is creeping up behind). Writer tells the truth about the Twin Towers conspiracy; author writes novel while kidnapped by Brazilian pygmies in the rain forest: anything which will attract an actual headline. At the very least something set in a five-star hotel in a hot and steamy holiday resort popular with the Royals. That's for the magazine market. It's all niche marketing nowadays. Don't neglect the elderly. Seventy-year-old grandfather accused of abuse writes novel in prison, daughter commits suicide as a result: that one's been serialised on Radio 4. Can we have more like that? Simple romance is always fail-safe but not too steamy. Propriety is in, Erotica is out. *Fifty Shades of Grey* somehow exhausted that market. Middle-aged women make up most of the book market but prefer their heroines young enough to be sexy because they like to identify. Dystopias are all the rage but not if it's too clever. No-one wants satire, there's no market for it. Readers have gone off smartness: wise to leave comedy for stand-up comics, it can go so wrong. Ghost stories: iffy. Paranormal – too niche-market for comfort.

I oversimplify, I know I do: on the whole good books get published and bad books don't. But it's really hard to sell books, so give Marketing a chance. If you're the one who wrote the North London book, you might have got a better reception if you'd actually mentioned that Jasper is a deaf mute and/ or Aramintha an asylum seeker, and cited that and not your elegant metaphors to the editor as being at the heart of the novel. Marketing have been known to boast that they've never actually read a novel – they don't have the time. They rely on readers' reports and editors who pitch verbally.

Don't worry too much about your USP: no-one ever gets it right. Even Marketing. Especially Marketing, who often get it wrong. They know well enough what happened in the past but have no idea what will happen in the future. A few, mind you, and some publishers too, are just better than others at sniffing out what will happen next.

All the same, you can always try surprising yourself after six rejections: open by sending your characters off to North Korea on holiday, or writing the same novel from the man's point of view not the woman's – the abandoned man not the abandoning woman – or the villain's viewpoint not the victim's.

Everything may suddenly leap to life. You're the writer: it's your universe, you can do anything.

Back in 1933 someone once wrote a whole novel without using the letter 'e' and got away with it. It was in the present tense. You could get rid of the 'ed's that way. He had to self-publish, mind you, but it made quite a stir.

f) It's too controversial

It's easy enough for this to happen. Novels take a long time to write. The novel you started five years ago might seem rather unfashionable today. Perhaps you're writing a thriller and have made all the baddies Muslim, when these days it seems mandatory to make them 'far-right'. You may have culturally appropriated a black rape victim when you might just as well have made her white; or made an unseemly joke about gender fluidity; or been too forgiving of a paedophile. The patterns of social disapproval change furiously and fast and having to point it out to the writer can be embarrassing for all concerned. Easier for them to just say 'no, not for us'. It's as much awkwardness as deliberate censorship.

If you suspect you're too controversial, you have various options:

1) You can seek out a brave publisher and approach them directly, bypassing the agent.
2) You can wait for society to see it your way and your views to be welcomed (could take twenty years).
3) You play safe, act Vicar of Bray (Google him) when you rewrite, adjust to contemporary requirements, and re-submit. It may be easier than you think. Find a white church-goer amongst the rapist gang, make the terrorist a mental health victim, the alleged molester falsely

accused, and that may be all you need to achieve balance. Don't blame me if you get bored or furious doing so; you do want to get your book published, don't you? And you don't want a troll storm raging around your poor creative head.

g) Your synopsis failed to explain your novel

A modern-day synopsis isn't just a convoluted, hard to follow and ultimately boring account of the plot. Martha did this and William did that, and then this, that and the other happened. Not enough. Your synopsis, together with your letter of introduction, needs to give an overview of your novel – the genre, why you wrote it, what you see as your potential market, and any other special thing you want to say in your novel's favour. Keep it brief, professional and business-like. Keep it to a page. Agents will use it when they pitch it to publishers; publishers when they sell it internally, as these days they have to do. Be positive about what you've written but avoid boasting. (Agents and publishers are no different from you; they can tell blarney when they see it.) By all means tell them you hope your book will be a favourite amongst cat lovers, not that it's the most brilliant novel about cats ever written. They like to be the judge of that.

Surprisingly few people will read all your novel. The first six pages of actual text is usually enough for an accomplished literary agent to see a novel with potential and put it aside for a 'proper read'. If they're a new young 'rights agency' – there are more and more of these about – and think your novel sufficiently plot-rich to have a future on TV or film, they will say 'well perhaps, but first just alter it to meet our specifications'. Be very careful because sometimes they are right but sometimes they are wrong. I have known writers take a year or more doing as an agent suggests and at the end of it they still say 'no, not for us'. Because what they think 'worked' just didn't when it came to selling it to anyone, least of all a 'serious' publisher with properly trained, experienced and responsible staff.

You were so grateful to have been singled out you didn't notice the warning signs that this particular agent was new at the game, inept and irresponsible, all three. Writers should never be too grateful. Also, people change. I have been at this game for fifty years: I have known beloved and trusted agents run off to South America with the money, turn to drink, to cocaine, to die. I have known accountants be struck off, lawyers hang themselves. We're all only human, and don't go on forever.

h) Too much fine writing, too little plot?

This too can happen. You've been a natural writer

since you took up a pen. Teachers have marvelled at your skill with words, the beauty of your prose, your astonishing gift for metaphor and so on. It's not just your mother who thinks you are wonderful, but colleagues and established writers who wish they could write as well as you. But the fact is you're not a novelist, you're more of a poet, though since you write to the end of the line you haven't realised it.

Structure, plot, doesn't come naturally to you. After a page or so of admiring your fine writing readers may well feel *'that's enough of that for now'*, put the book down thinking *'but I wanted a story'*, and somehow not go back to it.

If this applies to you, don't trust your novel to develop naturally, to grow by itself – it won't. Construct a plot before you begin – get help if required – and stick to it resolutely. Don't let yourself wander off, however tempted, however intoxicated by your own words.

i) What do they mean 'illiterate'?
How dare they!

'Poncy bastards! Sheer elitism. I'm of the people, speak like the people, spell like the people. I have a story to tell and haven't I told it? Grammar and spelling? Who cares! Someone up at the publishers can attend to all that, they have the computers! (How am I expected to pay for one, I'm on benefits?) Bet they did all the corrections for *The Curious Incident of the Dog in the Night-Time*.'

Well, yes, probably. But that book had other merits. And any errors were intentional anyway. Perhaps yours were too? If so, tone them down. If not, and you suspect this is the reason for rejection, then learn the ways of the over-educated, if only because they are the ones who buy the books. Not everyone who succeeds has been to creative writing classes. Start by reading novels, the more the better. Consult the FAQ section in Part Four of this how-not-to handbook. And consider film making, where the use of words can become an irrelevancy and you can get your story out and stop it driving you mad.

Part Two

No-one knows anything, but trust is important

A word about cockroaches: Kurt Vonnegut suggested that readers should be so aware of what was going on in a novel they would not worry 'if cockroaches ate the last few pages'. I'm not sure I agree. All kinds of things can happen in the last few pages, though you have to avoid the vulgar twist which is a feature of old-fashioned short stories. *Gone Girl* ends (spoiler alert!) with a major reversal of expectation – the murderous psychopath Amy is pregnant and yet will be allowed to live happily ever after. It's the baby one is left worrying for, considering its parents. Though come to think of it, perhaps it was one reversal too many, and some did quarrel with the way the novel ended.

As to the cockroaches, they do go nibble-nibble in their disgusting, cloacal way at paper (though we must, I suppose, remember we are all God's creatures) and the problem doesn't apply to the contemporary writer and her laptop, or the reader with her Kindle. But Vonnegut laid down his rules for students at a time when there was a plague of cockroaches in New York. The creatures would fall from the ceiling into your dinner; pull back the bedclothes and find a whole swarm cavorting there. And they nibbled away at everything, darkly horrible and squashy if you trampled them.

Nowadays the metaphor would be devoid of drama – more to do with your Kindle crashing the page before last, as you read, and you not minding too much. And actually I would mind quite a lot, and feel fate was treating me unfairly if I lost the last few pages of anything I'd written, and the more clear and to the point I had managed to be, the more I would fret. Blank-screen panic would ensue. It scarcely happens with new computers, as technology advances, but upgrading is such a horrific experience one tends to put it off. When it does, be consoled. What is rewritten out of memory is sometimes so much better than the original work, it is as if fate had intervened not to ruin you but to save you.

Yes, I know: Pollyanna or Pangloss. But one can always hope.

Six rejections?
It really is too bad!

You'll have behaved properly. You'll have believed publishers when they said they didn't accept unsolicited submissions and you needed to find an agent. (They lie.) You'll have looked through the websites of the hundreds on offer, taken advice and chosen the agent you like the look of. You'll have done as they requested and sent a covering letter, the first chapter of the novel and a synopsis, and submitted electronically. (At least email is cheaper and quicker than snail mail. Learn to welcome the new paper-free world.)

At the beginning it felt discourteous to send it to more than one agent at a time – you didn't want to annoy – you know only too well it's a buyer's market: supposing they take against you? You clicked 'send' to your first choice. You waited weeks, months even, for the courtesy of a response and when (if) one came it was a brief and shocking 'not for us', sent off by someone you instantly suspect, possibly rightly, to be an unpaid and over-worked intern.

If you were lucky, the response came in the form of a rave rejection: 'we loved your book, so original, so witty, so wise', whatever, but still 'not for us'. So you start the whole submission process over again, by which time you've stopped worrying about manners and are sending four or five or more at a time to second-best agents chosen at random, like as not, from the several hundred in the *Writers'*

& Artists' Yearbook. When a couple of years later they're still 'not for us'-ing, and friends and family are getting sick of you and your novel, you give up and face facts. No-one wants your novel.

All the same, it's a humiliation. An apology might help you to forgive and forget, any indication of what you're going through, but it isn't going to happen, is it. Face it. You're caught up in the great maw of the publishing industry: just as twenty tons of rock and soil must be dislodged and discarded before a single gold ring can be made, so publishing rejects the great bulk of its raw material. The vast majority of submitted books get rejected, pulped, deleted, buried in landfill.

So now you have various options:

1) You can spend the rest of your life disappointed and aggrieved.

2) You can cheer up. Look, it wasn't for nothing. You will understand a great deal more about

yourself when it's done than when you began: you've managed to impose a beginning, a middle and an end on some small aspect of your existence, which is a great life lesson, the beginning of all wisdom, like giving birth to a baby. You'll have come to terms with the compulsion that required you to write the novel in the first place (very often related to your own childhood traumas, as I've pointed out before). Nothing has been wasted.

3) You can start a new novel – much easier second time round. Not a bad idea at all.

4) You can rewrite the first one, after due attention to its weaknesses, and re-submit. It will be hard and tedious work, and requires courage and faith, but I have known it succeed. Personally, I wouldn't submit more than six times without seeing if a little editing might not go amiss in order to improve my chances. See Part One.

If you have selected 1), just close this treatise and get on with your life, while realising that for the rest of it you will feel a sharp pang when anyone you know gets their book published. As Gore Vidal said, 'Every time a friend succeeds, something in me dies'.

Mind you, resentment can be quite invigorating: very little in this life being ever entirely bad or good. At least there'll always be something to complain about.

First of all, know your enemy

Not quite enemy, but do realise that though agents and publishers naturally present themselves as friends, they are actually colleagues. Read the small print. Your interests and theirs overlap but do not necessarily coincide.

As Sun Tzu said, in *The Art of War*: 'If you know the enemy and know yourself, you need not fear the result of a hundred battles. If you know yourself but not the enemy, for every victory gained you will also suffer a defeat. If you know neither the enemy nor yourself, you will succumb in every battle.'

Find out the basics – what exactly is a literary agency?

Should the agency take on your work it's in the hope, not the certainty, of finding you a publisher. They are talent scouts, the middleperson between you and your desired goal to appear in print. They normally enjoy good relations with acquisition editors and know where your novel is likely to find a home. They pitch your book and try to get you the best deal. It is in their best interest to negotiate lucrative contracts as they work on commission (usually 15 per cent of what you make). It is as well to have an agent – though a few prosperous writers use lawyers – since they manage your affairs with the publisher once the deal goes through. Do vet your contract to make sure you haven't given away more rights than you need, collect your money, keep records, settle contract disputes – leaving you on good terms with your editor at the publishing house and freeing up your time to write. The better you get on with your agent the easier life will be.

Be bold, be bold, but not too bold, is my motto. Argue, but never so much they throw you out the door.

So let's envisage the scene at, say, the Silk and Stone (UK) literary agency, when your novel rises to the top of the pile – an old-fashioned metaphor related to paper submissions which will soon enough find a digital equivalent – and is to be discussed. Samantha, Crystal, Carol and Agnes will be in the room with their laptops open, scrolling through the 'possibles'. (There might be a Tom in the room but it's less likely than it was, the gender balance in the lower ranks of today's publishing industry being what it is.)

Let's say for the sake of argument you have called your novel *Whither Charles?* – a bad, boring choice; they will hate it. It is about a dentist in Leeds called Charles whose wife discovers he's having an affair and is trying to send him mad and succeeds. A kind of reverse *Gaslight*, but you didn't say that in your synopsis, instead rather rashly describing it as a mixture of Strindberg's *The Father* and Edvard Munch's *The Scream*.

Agnes is the one who first opened the submission, seven weeks after it pinged up on the agency website. (Silk and Stone are a conscientious agency and usually send out notice of receipt immediately, but lately, what with 'flu and pregnancies, have found themselves understaffed so this practice has rather gone by the board. They're doing what they can. But then everyone does what they can.)

Agnes read the first seven pages and the synopsis: put it into the 'possible' file. Agnes is ageless and in charge. She's clearly top totty; a double first from Oxford, elegantly skinny, beautifully coiffed and clothed, with cropped hair, amazingly long, long legs and bright blue eyes. Age: uncertain. 'Ten possibles to discuss today,' she says now, 'and a limit of three to submit to our publishers.' (Agents tend to work with their favourite publishers. A lot of lunching goes on.) 'Unless something fantastic turns up, of course. So shall we get a move on? We'll begin with *Whither Charles?* At least this one's basically literate. It's a good rich plot, but unbelievable and with an inconclusive ending. I've no idea who's meant to be good and who bad. Let alone what genre it is. But does that matter?'

She describes the plot. Nice husband, dentist

Charles, is being driven literally mad by evil narcissist wife Clara just because he's having an affair with a fat mistress whom she murders by giving her an allergenic cat and shutting them both in the laundry room. Charles gets accused of the murder but fortunately can now claim insanity. Which Clara hadn't thought of. Thus everyone is possibly punished, or possibly not. The intern was asked to summarise the synopsis, which originally went on for six pages, but only managed to get it down to four. Nor has he done a good job in that half hour on the novel that took you four years to write.

'The writing's not good enough for a literary novel,' complains Samantha, looking through her notes. 'And it's an uncertain genre, so yes, it matters.' Samantha is rather shorter and rounder than Agnes, but still expensive. She is twenty-seven, known to be brilliant and extra literate, has a 2:2 from Leeds (too busy politicking to do any better), a property developer boyfriend, and has just put down the deposit on a flat in Hackney. She has long black hair, mildly druggy eyes, a fringe which gets into her eyes, and pimples round her chin, which one hopes can't be from glue sniffing. She's pregnant and wishes she wasn't.

'Possible sale to TV, I suppose,' Samantha goes on. 'But plonk, plonk, plonk, the writer goes, and her stereotypes move around like robots. She says it's a thriller but where's the thrill? And hopelessly naïve, PC-wise: all that stuff about adorable male buttocks and sucking quims! Meant to be sexy but just isn't. Out of the ark. I hated it from the first page and fell asleep. No way I can stand in front of someone from acquisitions and enthuse. I'd be a laughing stock. Abort, abort!'

Agnes: 'Thank you, Sam. At least that's definite. Anyone else?'

Crystal: 'I think Sam's being rather hard. There are still some women out there who fancy a mean male arse. But I found myself reading on, in spite of not wanting to. Of course they're all stereotypes. Isn't that the point? Easy reading? The new Dan Brown, perhaps? Get her to change the end and sell it to Marketing as a reverse psychological thriller – woman plots to murder man; it usually being the other way round. She'll have to take out the boiled cat found in the hottest wash. Too many cat lovers out there. But I don't mind having a go. Stodgily written but Marketing might not notice. Plot is all.'

Crystal came out of Springfield High when she was sixteen with a GCSE in English and all the rest fails but was so competent as an intern she was kept on, and thrived. She understands the zeitgeist: knows what she likes and likes what she knows.

Agnes (who doesn't think plot is all): 'Thanks, Crystal, very helpful. Carol?'

Carol: '"Might" is not good enough, Crystal. And you try getting this author to change anything! Not if she thinks she's Strindberg and Munch combined. And wasn't Munch some kind of artist anyway? She can't be very bright. If you did try to edit, she'd only put the baby in the wash instead of the cat and make the mother watch it go round and round. No, she'd be real trouble as a client. This agency simply can't afford to spend too much time persuading difficult clients to rewrite. And it's about a dentist. Dentists never work. By the time I'd read the synopsis – I never got to see any summary – I was exhausted. So I must admit I didn't read much of the text. But she spelt "necessarily" wrong in line three.'

Carol is the daughter of the CEO of Silk and Stone (US) and is, like Agnes, on the UK Board. She's also on IVF and has been for four years and still no success.

Samantha rushes for the loo feeling suddenly nauseous, so everyone waits for her to return. If she doesn't, *Whither Charles?* might still stand a chance. If a slim one.

Morning coffee is brought in by the intern, a lad

straight out of uni with a BA in Creative Writing. No-one can say Silk and Stone (UK) don't try to create gender balance. There is no coffee, but herbal teas, nut bars and pumpkin seeds. Caffeine is a no-no. Everyone is on a diet. Samantha is a long time away.

Whither Charles? is put on hold: a novel called *Cloning with Claude* is dismissed as too obscure and a misery memoir called *The Light that Failed* is accepted, Crystal having convincingly argued that it would appeal to any publisher of large-print books, though she has a vague unease about the title. Didn't Kipling use it, or someone?

Samantha rushes back in and says she's having a miscarriage. She suspects the image of the baby drowning in a washing machine is to blame. By implication this is Carol's fault. Sam has taken off her five-inch heels and looks wretched and desperate and her white leather skirt is bloody. 'Perhaps it's just as well,' she says, bravely smiling.

Carol snorts. An ambulance is called: the meeting breaks up. The intern uses his discretion as he is always being urged to do, though usually gets into trouble when he does, puts *Whither Charles?* in the Reject file, and it's forgotten.

'Not for us' goes out a month or two later. Silk and Stone (UK) are even more understaffed than usual.

This is a worst possible case, but I had fun writing it, and these things happen.

If it has, don't give in, *take steps*.

But what happens if you're a man in this feminised world?

All at agency and publisher will claim that their choices are gender-neutral, and this is probably the case. Those in these offices will all 'love books' and 'meeting authors', or claim to, but all have to make a living somehow. Profit is profit, 15 per cent of the gross that you, their client, earns is not to be sneezed at. Far more women write or read fiction than do men, but whereas men are reluctant to read female fiction (they fear infection by soppiness) women have no such reluctance when it comes to reading novels by men. They appreciate a touch of the macho, or perhaps it's just some lingering leftover from the first half of the last century when men were seen as the superior sex. So, if anything, the male as novelist has a slight advantage over the female, being more of a rarity, and so desirable. Fear not. Gender discrimination is the least of your worries.

Part Three

How to keep
the reader happy

Writing is such a peculiar thing to find oneself
doing in the first place – this unlikely urge to create
alternative universes. The novelist feels obliged to
do the work better left to the forces of evolution,
helping the Blind Watchmaker on His way, offering
yet more possibilities as He splits and divides, splits
and divides His nuclei – this one's temperament,
that one's physique – until perfection of the human
psyche is achieved and the asteroid strikes or the

earth falls into the sun. It's as if the Great Designer needed help from a handful of humans to think up yet further variations on His creation, or Her, mind you, or Zir, or whatever pronoun you prefer in these touchy days. It seems such a privilege to be declared a novelist, one had better teach: pass on what one has found out in practice about the rules of the craft, the guild, the discipline, the calling, however one sees it. So let us examine the accepted rules of writing novels, and a few of the rule over-rides for when the former break down. Which they often do (this is often called genius).

The rules and
non-rules of writing

Sticking to the accepted rules is not a silly thing to do, though many a novelist spurns the idea and gets away with it, and just as well, or nothing in writing would change or develop. Which has not stopped many a great writer inventing and listing them.

Kurt Vonnegut did it, as did Elmore Leonard, Stephen King and E.M. Forster – in *Aspects of the Novel* (1927) – and many another. It seems obsessional of them: but such a delight when they got it right. Their skill demands to be handed on.

Kurt Vonnegut (1922–2007) was an American author who wrote fourteen novels, three short story collections, five plays and five works of non-fiction in his lifetime. I am a great fan, if only because reading Vonnegut's novel *Slaughterhouse Five* (1969) taught me how to be adventurous, how to get out of the house, how to leap about on the page in time and space to good purpose. If you get bored with yourself, so will the reader: so just cut as a film editor does, set up your next scene and move on.

Vonnegut was one of the first to realise that creative writing was a teachable subject, so long as you regarded it as a craft, not an art. You can't teach people *what* to write, but you can make a fair bash at teaching *how* to write. He saw the reader as a stranger whom you need to make your friend, using all the ingenuity you could, as soon as you could. Writers were the servants of their readers, not the other way round. If they wanted to be read they had to learn humility, and not annoy.

On finding your subject

Your reader is a stranger: you know nothing about her or him as an individual, so even before you start writing look for something you have in common with others. You have the whole human condition to work from, namely, that we are born, we love, we dream, we hope, we grow old and we die. So think big. Find a subject you care about and which you know others care about too, and if they don't, know that you'll persuade them to. Make this discovery your mission statement, your cosmic sentence, your plea to the universe (agree with me! Please agree with me. I'm right!). Shape it in your head in words, then stick to it. That energy, that conviction, will be the most compelling and seductive element in what you end up writing, not the ingenious and startling way you play about with language.

Please, please, in other words, just say what you

mean and leave the stage. Don't ever use three words when one will do: keep it simple.

It helps to have your cosmic sentence before you start – see Part One (b) and (c) – but some writers just start writing and cover pages, chapters even, before they realise what their novel is about. It may come to them as a shock of understanding. Then quite a lot of rewriting and restructuring will be required, but the unease and the doubt stop. All writers work differently, which is why I say there are no rules, just non-rules, not just for genre fiction (where they are more obvious) but literary fiction as well.

Having found it, keep it simple

'Keep it simple,' said Elmore Leonard. 'That is my motto in life.'

'Simplicity of language is not only reputable,' wrote Vonnegut, 'but perhaps even sacred.'

Once you have decided what you are doing, use clean, short words everyone understands. Be as clear as you can. Don't hide the names of your characters. Don't write 'endeavour' when you can say 'try', or write 'crepuscular' when you can say 'twilight'. Don't be afraid of full stops, or 'said's; go easy on the adverbs and adjectives and steer clear of the passive voice. Your readers will salute you for saying what you mean and meaning what you say.

Honour your readers. You're asking them not just to spend money on your book, but to spend hours of their time reading it. Time is far more valuable than money, and it could be spent on actually living rather than reading. Take the readers more seriously than you take yourself. Don't waste their time. Make sure they close your book satisfied, feeling their money is well spent. Don't try to make them admire you. You simply want to be seen as a friend who has never annoyed them. Then they'll buy your next book. You have the craft of writing at your fingertips:

use it to the best of your ability to transfer what is in your head into that of your reader, by virtue of (Vonnegut's words) *'making people laugh or cry about little black marks on sheets of white paper'* because that's all words are.

And always bear in mind the advice of the seventeenth-century Japanese samurai, guru Musashi, in *The Book of Five Rings* (circa 1645) – 'Do nothing that is of no use.'

Puzzle bad, suspense good

Don't hide information from the reader. It is really annoying. Give them what they need to know as soon as they need it. Don't try and mystify them. This is the non-rule I spend most time discussing with my students, and the one with which they have most difficulty.

'But I thought a novel had to have suspense,'

the student says. 'Surely one needs to worry about what is going to happen next. It's why the reader wants to turn the page. It's what I pride myself on doing.'

'There's a difference between suspense and puzzle,' I say. 'And what you are doing is puzzle – there's nothing more annoying for a reader than having to flick back through the pages to work out what on earth's been going on, or who was speaking.'

'Yes, but I've been told in Eng. Lit. classes that's what the great writers in the canon do – hold people in suspense – and I should try and do the same.'

'But that applies to the whole book – *what on earth will happen next?* – not individual pages, let alone paragraphs, let alone sentences where you refuse to even give your characters names or tell us what they look like or what they do, in the sorry belief that readers are longing to find out. They're not. You've given them no reason to. And anyway that was then, when readers had servants and time on their hands, and this is now, when they haven't. Readers just want you to get on with it and not play games. Please do not try and write a great novel, just a good and saleable one. "Great" is for others to judge, not you to aspire to.'

'Yes, but—'

'I know your "yes, buts",' I reply, 'from having read Eric Berne's great book *Games People Play* about people's compulsive tendencies (essential reading, by the way, for anyone writing a novel). Patterns of thought; justifications which stop people from getting on with their lives. And not just other people's either. Writers are good at "yes, buts", as they resist tuition. But like anyone else they have bad habits, irritating patterns of expression which are referred to as fidgets.'

'But I've always written like this!'

'I know. That's why no-one has so far published

you. Stop it. You annoy agents and editors as well as readers by mystifying, so they can miss the whole point of an otherwise good novel. Just speak straight and clear. Do that and your reader will trust you and pay attention, seeing that you have something to say and are proud of it. Again, stop trying to be a great writer and see yourself as someone trying to write a novel that readers want to read and so will sell.'

'Yes, but—'

'Oh please! Time's up, anyway.' And the tutor closes the door after the student rather too sharply.

The only time a writer can afford puzzles is when writing a detective story, when there is an acknowledged game going on between reader and writer, a contract, and the overall suspense lies in which of you is going to get the solution first. Otherwise, steer clear. Not for nothing are detective stories called 'mysteries'.

You, the writer, are in command but must show

mercy. Treat the reader as your best friend, not your enemy. Don't challenge them to love you.

Take advice from the film and TV world

Make at least one character likeable – otherwise people close your novel saying, 'But everyone was so perfectly horrible.'

The reader really wants to read about himself, herself: so make it possible. Have one admirable person amongst your den of thieves, one firm apple in the barrel of bad soggy ones. Keep your characters psychologically plausible – that is to say miserable and screwed up from time to time by all means, but a few simple good folk on the page do not go amiss. A reader likes to identify: what happens to *me, me, me*? 'Me' is what keeps him or her turning the pages. Acknowledge the flaws your protagonists have, give them a few trivial worries to overcome while they get on with their heroism; let your heroine worry about losing weight, your hero about getting it up: nothing wrong with a wounded hero. Let your unhappy endings be few and your happy endings be many: or else, fearing depression and bad news, readers – like film or TV viewers – will flee.

Make your goodies and baddies easy to spot. This can be done in the first few frames in a film so that everyone knows the score. The goodie rescues the kitten from the branch, or the baddie kicks the cat out of the way. This is simple for screenwriters, more complicated for novelists. Screenwriters have actors, directors, cinematographers, designers to pave their way. Everything is show rather than tell. The first few frames show the viewers everything they need to know, other than the actual story. Age, looks, social status, setting. Music and lighting define mood. Before the actors even open their mouths viewers can see for themselves all the things the writer is condemned to describe or infer – gender, race, looks, age, class, income, education – before the story proper can begin. It is amazing how often young writers who've been reared on fiction unfolding on a screen forget to address these things, have to be reminded that scenes have to be set, people have to be described, backgrounds delineated, before readers have a hope of following what is going on.

It helps to make the person you want your reader to relate to likeable. Even Kafka's black beetle had his good points. No-one wants to spend too much time with people or creatures they don't get on with. See your novel as a bedtime story writ large and long. The child wants to go to sleep feeling that when the light goes out, some order has been made of an otherwise chaotic universe. The good have been rewarded and the bad punished.

The wise psychologist Donald Winnicott saw the bedtime story as another of the small child's 'transitional objects' – like the old piece of blanket the toddler wails and wails for if any attempt is made to part them. The parent dare not get a word wrong when the familiar story is retold, because, Winnicott says, the child is busy working out the difference between reality and illusion. The adult novel is another, more complicated, version of the bedtime story in which right is rewarded and wrong punished: the story we all want to hear, in which heroes win out and heroines find true love. Novels are lucky charms: the little rectangles of compacted paper covered with littler squiggles of black and white we carry about next to our hearts on trains and in quiet living rooms and hate to be parted from. Finish one, start another. Or even write one of your own.

The child returns again and again to Pooh or Horrid Henry or Curious George or Orlando the Marmalade Cat, or, growing older, to the bespectacled Harry Potter. All vanquish their enemies, are us yet are not us. Remember this while you write, solve your readers' moral dilemmas for them and they will be grateful. Reward the good, punish the bad, and you will have returned at least some reassuring order to a chaotic universe.

You are in charge

Don't let your characters run off on their own. That's weakness, not something to be proud of. Keep them on track. They all want something, otherwise they wouldn't be in your novel at all. Decide what it is they want before you set out on this 80,000–120,000-word journey with them. Will you give them it or won't you? Let them pay you proper respect. You may be the reader's servant but at least the characters are yours.

Your main characters need to want something important – whether success or true love, revenge or forgiveness, peace of mind or excitement:

86

should their desires conflict so much the better. Then you can spend the whole middle of the novel working out their predicament. You can either give them what they want (happy ending) or deprive them of it (unhappy ending) but your readers will identify the more, care the more. See how minor characters will come to life if you give them needs. Let the postman who trudges through the snow to deliver a writ to the door desire new boots, let the passing hill-walker be thirsty for a glass of water. Your characters will then not live in isolation but in a real, albeit fictional, world.

People your novel with needy characters who will then seem familiar to your readers. Feel generous both towards characters and readers. It may be only an extra sentence or two out of your busy writing life, or the odd adjectival phrase, but it's energy and life to the extras who wander in and out of your novel. Let the readers see what these people are feeling and doing. And remember to remain observant in your fictional universe: see what the sky and the sea look like, the local flora, feel the hot days, shiver in the cold, taste the food, long for a cigarette, even give them a cold in the nose from time to time.

Always remember, readers miss things. They don't necessarily read every word you write, more's the pity. Writers write steadily along the line, word by careful word, and assume readers read the same way. But readers don't, or do only if they're still children mouthing the words. Adult readers absorb words in blocks of text, noticing unusual or unexpected ones, making sense of those, and passing over what is obvious and expected.

The brain plays strange tricks at the best of times. Try counting the number of 'f's there are in the following sentence: 'Finished files are the result of years of scientific study combined with the experience of years.' You probably said three or four. Actually there are six. You simply did not notice all the 'of's. So don't rely on the reader to pick up every single thing you have said. And do remember that readers *miss* things. Should you head your chapters with a year date, few will ever notice: so make sure you repeat it in the text. And by the way, readers notice words with two 'zz's in them. A dazzle or a drizzle, a sozzle or a sizzle always get attention. Use this knowledge judiciously.

A good book takes longer to read than a bad one. While you can skim through *Fifty Shades of Grey*, Thackeray's *Vanity Fair* takes longer page for page. Why? Is it that 'bad' writers are dealing with the obvious, 'good' writers with the unexpected – so the mind takes longer to work out what is going on? Is it that the minds of the former are not worth following but the latter are? And why in any case are we differentiating between good and bad? Good bad books have their place in the world. I'm not knocking them: we need our entertainment, our relief from grim reality – sometimes we just don't want to think about reality too much. Bad good books are worst of all – they're unreadable and won't sell any copies.

But good books count as that mysterious thing, 'literature': they inform, absorb, hold you: they invite your emotional involvement, excite your intelligent participation and they are hard to forget. A pity that bad books (you can tell them because they're so littered with adjectives, adverbs and strong verbs – 'her lovely, glossy chestnut hair tumbled lazily etc. etc. as she dimpled suggestively up at him' – sell better than good books.

Oh well. Pity. But – so it goes, as Vonnegut would say.

Keep to the point

If a sentence doesn't cut the mustard – that is, it doesn't either set the scene, advance the action or tell us more about a character – what's it doing in your novel? Delete it. Sentences have to work for their existence.

It's no use you just 'expressing yourself', working out some private emotion of your own. You're writing a novel here. No-one wants to know about *your* hopes and fears, your likes and dislikes and the changes you want to bring about in the world, they want to know what will happen next to your protagonist, and how the *mise en scène* you started with develops.

Sure, write a (fairly) long description of a beautiful sunny day because that affects the mood of the character or how some action spoils it. Put in a whole political manifesto if you have to, if the detail is really relevant to your story. But don't just wander off into masses of irrelevant text – however much you admire your own writing (or if you're in some kind of workshop group, how good your friends and fans say it is). The section may be good if read out of context, but fitted into the whole it will just stick out like a sore thumb. Try to keep as much as you can in chronological order. In order to write the events of today you need to have written what happened yesterday. They will alter today.

Please remember you are writing a whole novel; not just the juicy parts of a novel. If you cherry pick scenes out of their natural order, you will end up in trouble. It's like eating all the icing from the top of a cake and then realising the icing had been holding the cake together and now it's crumbled. It will take forever fitting all the slices together in the right order, getting the time sequences right, not repeating yourself or leaving things out and having to read and re-read, cutting and pasting and getting things wrong. Believe me, I know, I've done it. I did it in a novel called *Splitting* so perhaps it was appropriate, but it wasn't half exhausting. The German writer Goethe once remarked that you could take a fly to pieces to see how it worked but when you put it together again it just didn't fly. Quite so. Start with the first chapter, please, and grow your novel out from there as something organic, which will flourish and bloom. Eventually, like all things, it will be closed and die but it was good while it lasted. Bearing the end in mind can be a problem if you don't yet exactly know what the end is, but even if you're simply making it up as you go along (and many a novelist has been known to do this) trusting your right-brainy unconscious too much, and denying your logical, rational, left-brainy side can be a dangerous business.

At the same time, refrain from deleting any strange and wayward sections that have unexpectedly come to mind. 'What was all that about?' you may wonder. But just in case it is your unconscious talking to you (that old thing; should it even exist, which many a neurologist denies. I mean where exactly in the brain can it be?), sneak these sections into an offcut file when your left-brain editor is looking the other way. Or better still, move them to the end of your document so when you finally get, triumphantly, to 'The End' – there they are, waiting for a final decision. They may illuminate your whole novel, as a powerful dream can illuminate what is going on in your life (rather than the other way round, as Carl Jung pointed out).

If it's me, I may well have a whole page of stray sentences and sections which I thought at the time I could do without. Over-egged, under-written, awkward, rash, embarrassing – whatever. Mostly I will have dealt with their substance already, one way or another, but occasionally it still seems a pity to lose them. So back they go. But mostly one deletes, so pleased one is to have arrived at 'The End', written those magic words. Writing a novel can feel like running a marathon. Reach the end tape and find yourself collapsing in relief.

The same thing with 'foreshadowing'. If an idea jumps in to surprise you by coming before you've consciously thought of the thing that's going to happen next, this unexpected and unsought shadow looms, don't ignore it – just in case, as I say, your deep unfathomable unconscious knows more about the plot than you do. Jot it down, consider it. Could it work? It may even be what's been missing all the time.

Novelists, I do believe, are not quite like other people. When in the throes of invention, conscious and unconscious can become indistinguishable as they pound the stuff out; the ink on the pen splutters, the typewriter ribbon splits, the letters on the keyboard wear out as writerly fingers bash away, litter builds up around them and they take no notice. Technology changes but the desire to explain the world to yourself and others doesn't. Sometimes it even feels it's all coming from some source other than you. All the same, it's a foolish writer who will admit to 'channelling'. It sounds far too New Agey for comfort.

The use and abuse of dialogue

Keep dialogue as brief as you can for this reason: dialogue is the writer's Achilles' heel, where revealing character and/or advancing action can sound forced and artificial. Unless your character is talking to a psychiatrist, a therapist or a housing officer, or anyone who is paid to listen, long stretches of uninterrupted speech are untenable.

Look especially hard at any dialogue scene which begins with a 'hello' and ends with a 'goodbye', when all you have in between is direct speech. It's surprising how many writers find themselves falling into this trap. The scene may take up two or three pages but when you read it aloud it will take as many minutes, so don't sandwich the scene between the 'hello' and the 'goodbye'. Cut the scene internally. Give your characters something to do which takes up time – go for a walk, bath the dog, make the dinner, burn the toast. Pick up the dialogue only when it gets interesting. And do use reported speech when things get tedious. Writers will take up a whole page having their characters decide where to meet next. It's boring. Just say 'They agreed to meet under the station clock a week from today, by which time his divorce papers would have come through,' and be done with it. The shorter the better, and the sooner you're going to get to your longed-for goal – The End. You are not being paid by the word: keep it brief.

As soon as you write 'hello' on a doorstep you're in trouble. There are the introductions, the hanging up of coats, the cups of tea, and the settlings down to endure. Don't put yourself through it. No 'hello's. Boring, unless someone's armed or carrying a writ. Cut into the middle of the scene, at the point where something of interest is being said. A 'goodbye' is safer, if accompanied by a slamming of a door.

Read aloud any scene which you've started with

'hello' and ended with 'goodbye'. Two pages will take you only two minutes to read, but will probably have taken hours in your characters' lives. Then look for solutions. 'Sipping his wine' (even though you give a history of the wine with its vintage and cost, and thus throw light upon the nature of the household where such drink is offered) is not enough. Similarly 'drinking her tea' is mere temporising, padding, and adds nothing. 'After she'd gone upstairs to get dressed' uses up more time. 'Arranged for the baby sitter to come round' is better still. And do remember that you can cut into the middle of scenes so that the passage of time is unspecified: 'Only after the Doberman had been fed and watered and they had settled down into their cups of rare Oolong tea and exchanged pleasantries did he say:…' will save you and your readers ten lines of boring direct speech, every word of which will have increased their doubt as to whether people do actually speak the way you've made them speak.

Where to start your novel

Graham Greene said use your intuition: 'A story has no beginning or end: arbitrarily one chooses the moment of experience from which to look back or from which to look ahead.' In *The End of the Affair* he was telling us how he himself thought through the voice of one of his characters: 'So much of a novelist's writing [...] takes place in the unconscious; in those depths the last word is written before the first word appears on paper. We remember the details of our story, we do not invent them.'

If you are not so confident in your own work, nearest the end is probably best. Your novel may cover a period of five years – but start it four years and fifty weeks in, and you will help yourself. 'Something happening' is what novels are all about, give readers the promise of it as soon as you can. Counsel of perfection: let your novel start with what happens one Saturday and end it on the following Saturday, by which time the problem you set up has been solved for good or bad, and the conflicts of years – brought to our attention by way of back story – have been resolved. (Keep the back story chronological or your reader will get confused.) Your reader will stay with you with bated breath for the few hundred pages in between, and then close the book with a satisfied 'Oh, I see' – waiting for the next book you write, having waited for a good two hundred pages to see how that initial scene would work out and having trusted you to resolve it. And you didn't resolve it in a single liner, either, did you? That will work for short stories – the twist at the end – but a novel needs a well-paced and considered scene which you have been working towards throughout the novel, in which the knots of all its strands can finally be untangled.

And please, please, as I keep saying, don't wilfully keep facts from your reader. Don't trust them to keep in their heads some mystery you have hinted at but not yet explained. They won't like you for it. Play it straight. If you're writing out of a character's head, remember you're not in a position to censor what is in that head. If your protagonist murdered someone years ago, it will crop up in his train of thought, as a source of anxiety, indifference or guilt. It will annoy your reader if having hidden the fact you then use it as a plot point.

And remember the convention that only one person in the scene has the feelings and reactions – and that's the one out of whose eyes events have been unfolding. He or she will only know what is going on in others' heads by observing their reactions. All others must be seen to react. Thus: *'At this news Bill felt a pang of fear. He saw Edward turn pale and realised that he too was frightened.'* Bill only knows what comes to him through his senses. This is a convention which people break all the time, but be aware of it.

Make something drastic happen

It would be possible to fit a whole novel in between someone putting the milk on the stove and it boiling over, to have the saucepan either snatched away in time, or not – but there are easier ways of making your readers pay attention. Let volcanoes erupt, memory be lost, war divide families. Do always try and get out of the kitchen, out of the house.

Just don't disappoint your readers. They have bought your book, preferred your company to their own, or they hope they will now they've handed over their hard-earned money. At stake is not just money; they are trusting a patch of their precious life to you. That is really flattering. The readers want a little relief from their own life – whether too boring, tragic or troubling – so do them proud. They want something from you that their own life isn't offering, be it entertainment, explanation, understanding, sympathy, fellow feeling, a sense of order and of justice. Real life is chaotic and without apparent meaning. Fictional life is ordered, structured and finite. 'The End', you write, and that's that, safely locked up and put away: an alternative universe understood and completed, one to treasure. The stronger the events in it the better. Blow up the volcano, join them on holiday in North Korea, set the whole thing in a submarine, just get out of the house. Agents will love you.

Of course you're going to express yourself one way or another but do it tactfully. Hard sell won't work, only your art of gentle persuasion. Of course you want your reader to end up thinking and feeling and acting exactly like you do: just don't let it show.

The agents' party

This party where you meet the agent is likely to be full of would-be novelists like yourself (or you wouldn't have been invited in the first place), so there will be a lot of other people trying to bend the agent's ear. It's a buyer's market. He or she will not be as interested in your novel's fine literary quality as in its genre and its appeal to a particular market. Literary quality is an optional extra, though one I very much hope you are aiming for. You will say something like 'I am writing a psychological thriller set in a market garden which will appeal to the 65 per cent of readers who love gardening.' Or 'I am writing a novel about body image. It concerns a slim girl who can never forget that once she was fat. Anyone who's ever been on a diet will want to read it.' Or 'I am writing a novel from the viewpoint of a blind dog, based on recent research. It's really cheerful, and dog owners everywhere will be fascinated.' Or even 'My novel? Oh, it's mass market, about a love affair, perhaps better described as a liaison, between a pretty, masochistic girl and a handsome man with very sadistic tastes.' Only then go into the 'There's this man and she said that and he did this' detail, which is irrelevant until your novel is well on the way to the publisher's copy editor. The agent just wants to know broadly what its market is. *Fifty Shades of Grey* was on its third publisher before it was accepted, then got to the right market – crudely described as mummy-porn – and did very well indeed.

If you work out some such account of your novel and keep it in mind even as you write, it will keep you on track and remembering there is an actual reader at the end of the process. Also an actual agent. You might even have her as the one reader you aim to please. Vile commercialism, I know, but a writer has to pay the rent. And since you're at the same party as the agent, you probably do have quite a lot in common.

Finding out what your novel is about, not just what the plot is, can require some quite painful introspection. Why have you chosen to write this particular novel at this time in your life and no other? Have you chosen it to validate some obsession of your own, whether it's 'I hate my mother and feel really bad about it', or 'I want to be revenged on climate deniers everywhere. I'll soon show them what's what!', or 'I deserved to be loved totally and overwhelmingly so why didn't you?' Whatever.

The story of the novel may well be your family story, however heavily in disguise, to yourself as well as others: the plot is the sum of the events that prove your point. Understanding your story is what keeps your plot on track, and the reader hooked, which is why it's important not to go wandering off into irrelevancies. Stick to the point. Irrelevancies may be torrid, erotic or lyrical scenes which flatter your literary skill and so charm and please you, but you lose your reader, who's trying to follow your story.

Be business-like. See yourself as writing so many

novels in the future you could be in danger of running out of the source material. You only have so much life experience to call upon. Wise to eke out what you have. These random scenes and subplots may well belong in the next novel. Never delete – just keep them in an offcut file. You never know.

There's a whole wide world out there, of course there is, but wise novelists set out to cover just a little segment of it. Theirs is the power of invention, but if they're sensible they keep it flowing strongly between well-maintained edges, not breaking its banks and spreading wide and stagnant over adjoining fields to the annoyance of everyone around.

Do what you set out to do, stick to the point, cut to the chase: don't get diverted, don't try and write like anybody else. You are not the new Jane Austen, the new Henry Fielding. Your own recognisable style emerges by itself – a balance between your personality and your choice of words. Copy no-one. You are you and this is your book, your idea, your achievement. Be confident. So long as you get away with it you can do anything you want. Your novel. Your choice.

Good luck!

An historical perspective

A novel is anything you can persuade a publisher to print, or otherwise reproduce. You're not writing just to satisfy yourself; you want other people to read what you have to say. Somehow you have to get it to them. All kinds of conventions have grown up regarding length, structure, production values and so on of the novel, but they're all only the result of custom, practice and changing technology. Chaucer wrote *The Canterbury Tales* – a novel in rhyme – in the 1380s before books could be printed, and had to be copied out onto vellum by scribes. These copiers were mostly teenagers, it was laborious low-paid work, their level of skill varied, but enough of these manuscripts still exist to suggest that Chaucer was the equivalent of today's best-seller. The manuscripts themselves were presumably paid for at great cost by eager fans, as word got around in the court circles where Chaucer spent most of his life, as philosopher, scientist, diplomat, administrator, and to all accounts the equivalent of today's Poet Laureate under Edward III, Richard II and Henry IV. I don't know how those financial arrangements worked, or who paid for what, but I hope a fair share of the proceeds went to Chaucer. He, after all, occupied the moral high ground. Without the writer, nothing. But just before he died I fear Chaucer too was writing a 'complaynt to his purse' in an attempt to get Henry IV to renew his annuity. So it goes.

When Caxton with his printing press turned up some seventy years later *The Canterbury Tales* was one of the first things printed. It did very well. For the next couple of centuries the writer had the upper hand, paying the printer to produce his (mostly his) parable of life and times; how the profit was to be split between the two men was a matter of arrangement. (Men, please notice, women being too busy with child and home care – no contraception, washing machines or loos – to do much writing.) Over the years the printers became publishers, outsourcing the printing, demanding a greater and greater share of the profits, running up production costs to prove the necessity: so now novelists – seldom great at business or self-publicity – get only a small advance so they can live while writing the book, and then a royalty, dictated by the publisher and dependent on how many are sold. The sum goes right down when and if your novel goes into paperback, by which time production costs have fallen greatly – and if for an e-book they are very little. So don't be too grateful when an agent or publisher condescends to buy your book. Remember it is a business transaction not some kind of blessing from the Gods. If they didn't think they'd make a profit from you they wouldn't publish you in the first place. Enjoy your lunch with them – they're some of the nicest, most glamorous and most fun people you'll ever meet (apart possibly from those in advertising) and will probably take you to a really good restaurant, but don't get carried away; always read the small print before you sign anything.

And don't think your novel has to be like every other novel published, so many pages in a certain house style, or believe canards such as 'nobody buys' novellas, or short stories, or will read your novel if it's written in iambic pentameters: it will sell if it's good enough. If you want to start a novel at the end and end at the beginning, you write it like that.

Take a lesson from Chaucer. He had no mentors, no accepted tradition to work from, no contacts made through creative writing classes. Chaucer's fame spread by way of handwritten manuscripts bought, lent and borrowed: he worked from first principles because there were no others to work from. Take a chance and invent a new tradition. He wrote in English (well, his own sort of English) at a time when the official language of the court was French, when the actual act of writing was massively more difficult than it is today. Vellum was expensive, ink was temperamental and difficult to acquire – goose quills were okay and cheap, but split and spluttered. The internet makes a book available by the million, Caxton only achieved thousands, the scribes a mere dozen or so.

Readers, I would suggest, don't much change over the centuries. They like a good simple robust story, a lot of sex, a hint of mortality, to be made to laugh, to be made to cry and with any luck, to think. So provide it.

Part Four

Frequently asked questions – a revision guide

Q) Why do I lose my way in the middle of a novel?
A) Because you've been ignoring the need for 'the story so far' breaks. Should you be in the middle of writing a novel it's a good idea to stop every now and then and devote a hundred words or so to writing down 'the story so far'. It focuses the mind on what you're doing and where you need to go next. It's all too easy to get lost in one's own verbiage, and the drive forward is lost.

'The story so far' at the beginning of each chapter serves as a reminder of where you are going and whence you have come. I know it's a counsel of perfection and the writer tends to resist – it seems a vulgar reduction to whittle down what you have been saying to mere plot, but it does help to keep you on track. Delete before delivering.

But careful – if you look back at what you have done so far and it feels like rubbish, resist the urge to delete and then empty the recycling bin. You may be wrong. You are Freud's toddler who looks at the poo in the pot, their own creation, and either cries out in disgust, 'Yuk, revolting!' Or else, marvelling, 'Did I create that out of nothing? Good Lord, I'm so wonderful!' So don't trust your own judgement, wait a day or two and look again, or you can always ask a friend.

The trouble with 'friends' is that they usually don't want to be asked, and if they do answer it's with any old thing the better to keep you quiet. Spouses are even less trustworthy. You may well have been censoring your work so as not to aggravate them, and supposing you failed? (I'm only half joking: it's a nervy job for a spouse, being married to a novelist who for all you know is spilling the beans about your private life, and keeps staring into space when you talk to them. Have pity, but don't necessarily trust their judgement.)

————

Q) Why do I have such trouble keeping to my synopsis?

A) Probably because your synopsis isn't worth keeping to. Your story has leaped beyond the bounds of its original 'and then, and then, and then' scenario. It's outgrown your initial 'he did this and she did that'. The plot you were so proud of has been overwhelmed by the story. Rewrite your synopsis, and not your novel.

———

Q) Why do you make this distinction between a plot and a story?

A) Because the plot – 'he's done this' and 'she's done that' – is just the mechanism by which you tell your story. The story is what you're trying to say, your plot the means of doing it.

By 'plot' I mean the events which move the story along: the 'story so far' rather like what you're shown at the beginning of an episode in a TV serial on Netflix. It brings you up to date with what's gone before, mood, characters, events and all. TV is heavy on plots, but in a good novel they're just the thread running through the whole: important, because it's what keeps the reader turning the page and wanting to find out what happens next. But other things are important too – characters have to change and develop as time goes along. It's not just 'and then, and then, and then'. You will be paying proper attention to your initial idea (the 'story' as opposed to just the 'plot') and remembering to keep to its point – and what your reader knows and doesn't know. You will be conscious too of form and structure; you will be using the resonance of language and grace of expression to heighten the impact of the story you are telling, the plot which illustrates it.

See your plot as what enables you to best express – by using event and character – what you are trying to say, the point you're trying to make. Which you can probably boil down into a single sentence. Such as 'All men are wicked', or 'Thus conscience does make cowards of us all', or 'Because someone's a victim doesn't make them nice', or 'Stepmothers are more to be pitied than stepchildren', or 'Having children is a real pain', or some other example of a cosmic statement. You need to make sure before you begin that your plot and your cosmic statement are not pulling in different directions. It's when they do that the task of writing gets laborious. All good novels have good plots, but a good plot alone does not necessarily ensure a good novel, for other factors intervene.

Be glad to be writing when you are. There are fashions in what makes a good novel. In 'literary' novels of the past plots were kept obscured: what happened to characters wasn't as important as what they thought and felt. 'Genre' novels – romance, sci-fi, thrillers – have only lately begun to get critical attention, more so perhaps due to the rise of the e-book, but all that's another story.

Of the novels in the canon that have come down to us from past centuries, many were written as serials. Perforce the reader had to remember them from month to month, even quarter to quarter. Plots had to be really evident. Characters had to be memorable. Each episode had to finish with a cliff hanger. Put the episodes together as a novel and you get Dickens, Thackeray, Conrad, Flaubert, Dumas, greatly respected now but at the time rather dismissed as commercial fiction, written with sales in mind.

Once upon a time, back in 1988, I was asked to write a serial for a leading women's weekly at the time – not a glossy, the opposite, with middle-market recipes, knitting patterns, advice on how to line the curtains and how to catch your man. Every week they'd carry two or three romantic short stories of a Mills and Boon flavour. Readers would check the end first to make sure it ended happily. Now the editor had the bright idea of a serial to fit the space in between the ads, either 1,000 words or 2,000, depending, to be delivered each week, to be published in the next weekly issue. He envisaged perhaps twelve episodes, starting as soon as possible. I said yes. And as it happened it ran for fifty weeks or so before the editor said, 'That's enough – my other writers are complaining you're taking up too much space.' It turned out to be a great training for me.

On a Thursday I'd get the early train up to London where my typist would be waiting (it was the days before the computer, let alone the internet), a two-hour journey – and write the episode by hand. The motorcycle messenger would call to collect at lunchtime. I allowed myself no time for editing or rewriting, let alone for second thoughts. A deadline is a deadline and has to be met. That was a year of no holidays, no illnesses, just all the discipline – and the fun, I must say – of *The Hearts and Lives of Men*, the title I gave it.

I think the editor must have thought the novel was already written and that I was doling it out meanly week by week, not that I was making it up as I went along. He would have been horrified if he'd thought about the mechanics of it. (So am I, in retrospect.) Or perhaps he wasn't thinking at all. But he never asked and I never told. Necessity, indeed, is the mother of invention, and we were all braver in those days.

It was only when I started to write that I realised the full structural implications of what I had committed myself to. I would have to start in the past or else I would end up writing in the future. It made sense to start with a child's adventures and grow the child up through the episodes. Dickens came to mind, of course. And the first sentence became *'Reader, I'm going to tell you the story of Clifford, Helen and little Nell.'* It's what I would call a Dear Reader novel; they're easier and simpler to write. The Victorians did it a lot. The Dear Writer becomes another character in the book – you can give her a personality which has nothing to do with you the real writer; you can digress at will and make comments on the way your characters behave. You can comment on the day's news or tell your heroine how to behave to win her man or how to improve her cucumber salad, all on the way to your cliff hanger ending. Which in an emergency, and I can tell you this piece of writing was full of emergencies

– air crashes and kidnappings and so on – were very useful. You could use up a whole 1,000 words in Nell's recollection of what had gone before, and then do a new cliff hanger ending in one line.

And every week there'd be a 'story so far' in the magazine to remind readers, and myself, what had gone before – just as in a TV serial you get the same developing intro every week using some old shots, some new ones. When you're writing, do think of ways of making things easy for yourself. Don't give yourself too many characters to deal with, too many subplots: solve the world's problems one at a time, not all at once. Remember you have a whole lifetime's writing ahead of you, leave some material in reserve for later on. And do bear in mind, especially in a course environment, that it's no use writing a series of 1,000-word pieces, no matter how brilliant, if they have no relationship with what went before. Writing 'the story so far' compels you to bear it in mind.

A 'McGuffin' was what Hitchcock called the mysterious object in a film that sets the whole chain of events into motion and can be used to bring it to an end. I had stipulated four weeks' notice before I got told to bring *The Hearts and Lives of Men* to an end, and had had the forethought to bring in my McGuffin at the beginning. I used a locket, worn by little Nell, kidnapped at the age of three, whose fortunes I was to follow until she was reunited with her parents some twenty years on. I could then, no matter what the circumstances were, prove her identity by producing the locket. These days you could simply use DNA, but not then. I had my cosmic statement buried in the second sentence: *'Helen and Clifford wanted everything for Nell, and wanted it so much and so badly their daughter was in great danger of ending up with nothing at all, not even life.'* So I had to keep putting Nell's life in danger as a result of her parents' inability to get on together, and 'the story so far' kept me on the straight and narrow.

When it was finished I simply left out 'the story so far's and it was published by Heinemann like any other novel. It is still in print, and very good reading it proves for patients in hospital whose lives are constantly being interrupted by X-rays, throat swabs and so forth.

All novels are written in different ways and all writers use different means to bring them about. The beginning and the end support a novel as the abutments support a bridge. Make sure they're firm and solid enough to support the structure. The bridge can come in all shapes; it just needs to get you across the water. See it as a structure, and don't let it get too thin in the middle. *The Hearts and Lives of Men* went on for so unexpectedly long I had to get Clifford and Helen to divorce and remarry in order to keep my McGuffin intact. An extra stanchion was required. But ingenuity will usually provide an answer.

In New Zealand in the thirties my father wrote a

detective serial for a magazine that went on for two hundred episodes before the editor asked him to bring it to an end. He had no idea by then who the murderer was. So he placed an advertisement in the newspaper offering a reward for anyone who came up with the answer. Someone did. Ingenuity pays.

———

Q) I'm still confused about structure. Tell me more?
A) All art forms have a structure. Basic rules apply. A novel's just two or three hundred pages covered with words unless it has a shape, a form. It can be full of characters and events, and people changing their minds (and so their fortunes), but without a structure it has nothing. Structure is different from plot and from theme, but is master of them both. It is the way you weave all the strands of your novel together to bring them to a satisfactory knot at the end. You don't have to feel oppressed: there are no

right or wrong ways, there are no fixed rules, it's just that the audience, your readers, needs to feel you know what you're doing: if they lose faith in you they will close the book. Equally your novel cannot be full of spelling mistakes or obvious errors: the reader has to trust you.

A novel is like a house: it can be built in all kinds of fashions and styles, but it has to have a roof to keep the rain out and windows to look out of. If the reader fears the roof is going to fall down she's going to get out of there as soon as possible. You've taken her money on false pretences. It may be a his, of course, not a her, but not so likely. There are twice as many female novel readers as there are male ones, and four out of five novel writers are women.

If you are writing within a genre, the rules of structure are tighter. You have to acknowledge them before you break them, in the same way a painter needs to know how to paint before he starts on abstraction. If you fail to solve a mystery in a detective story, it is only courteous to tell your reader near the beginning that there is no solution; if you are to make your romance end as tragedy, explain to the reader that this love affair is never going to work: if you are writing traditional sci-fi, apologise for bringing in human emotion.

Look up structure/novel writing on Google and a wealth of information is open to you. There are all kinds of interesting sites, offering advice. Take your pick. One writer describes the novels he writes as 'three disasters plus an ending'. Well, that's simple.

Someone else offers the suspension bridge image. Two pillars and a rope in between. At the first pillar you introduce your characters and their situation: one fifth of the way along you reverse the situation, two fifths the journey to a different destination begins – and so on. But you begin at the beginning and go on to the end: a simple 'and then, and then, and then' progression, providing a series of crises, bumps and humps along the way. This is the system favoured by writers of serials: Dickens, Thackeray, who start with their protagonists as children and then chart their adventures. If you are writing in a serial which is published as you go along, there is little alternative. You can't change your mind about anything. These writers use fiction to make their point – Dickens, the vitality of the working classes and the respect due to them; Thackeray, the vulnerability of the male to the ploys and foibles of the female.

The contemporary writer plays about with the timeline, tending to use any variation of the basic three-act structure. Act 1, Beginning – character and situation; Act 2, Middle – diversions along the way; and Act 3, End – climax and denouement. You can start your novel at any point, but must bring in the Act 1 material as soon as possible, and in Act 2, some foreshadowing from Act 3.

In a novel the beginning must be included in the end, the end in the beginning. That at least is fairly basic. Conceive your novel as a whole: not in detail but understand where you are driving. A novel, certainly one which has any ambition, needs to do a little more than just serve the genre; it needs to have a purpose as well as a plot. It may be useful to look at these websites and see what it is you're doing, less useful to use them as a guide to writing your novel.

Or there's 'Write your novel in 30 days', which seems too much like hard work to me. I rather favour the article method. You see your novel as a fictionalised article. You tell the reader what you're going to do (Act 1), do it (Act 2) and then (Act 3) tell them you've done it. You choose your characters and their conflicts to prove your point.

As for me, I see the novel as an act of persuasion, bringing the reader round to my point of view; but not every author would agree with me.

———

Q) Do agents prefer a happy or an unhappy end?

A) They don't mind, but you should. In the happy end the good are to be properly rewarded and the bad punished. In the unhappy end it's the other way round. Good idea to wait until almost the end to decide which seems most relevant. Do you want your reader to cry with sorrow or laugh with relief?

Either way a novel needs not just a shape, a beginning, a middle and a conclusion, but a purpose, a reason to write with which others will concur. You the writer – seen as more sensitive, more trained, more eloquent than ordinary mortals – have put your finger on something others have missed. You have 'something to say' and have said it, driving your point inexorably home, persuading others you are right to see the world the way you do. The more confident you are, the more eager the reader will be to read. (Do not deny an unhappy childhood – indeed the unhappier the better. 'Misery memoir' is a very saleable genre indeed, and Marketing people always like it.)

Readers interpret novels as confession and absolution rolled into one. Why else do any of us go round with this little rectangle of printed paper, this potted alternative universe as good as hung round their necks like a magic charm until exchanged for another, the better to get them through the day? 'I'm reading such a good book!' Can it be because increasingly, in a world without religion, when virtue must be its own reward, and we must live without a sense of divine retribution or heavenly compensation, when all experience is happenchance, and chaos and entropy rule, we look for certainties, for shape, for structure, for beginning, middle and some conclusion, however small, however brief – and this is the satisfaction the good novel brings us.

In our own lives, things happen without apparent reason or purpose, the good are not rewarded or the bad punished. Chaos rules. In the novel we witness a small patch of experience which makes sense, in which at least some kind of justice is apparent.

The child needs its bedtime story in just the same way, only simpler, not complicated by sexual desires. Bad snake gets punished, good rabbit gets rewarded. The craving for justice is the beginning of wisdom. (Heaven knows whence the child gets its 'It isn't fair' wail: there has been precious little evidence of it in his life.)

Gillian Flynn's *Gone Girl* is all about just deserts. Who was the guilty one, who the innocent? The novel tore away the surface of an outwardly happy marriage to show nothing but a pattern of lies, deceit and malice beneath. In her novel *Dark Places*, the brother massacres his entire family. Herself the most pleasant and mild of women, one does wonder what the hidden strains were in Flynn's own apparently happy childhood that still niggle so. We know her parents were academics – her father, a professor of film, took her to horror films when she was small, the better, no doubt, to discuss plot and structure; her mother taught literary comprehension at college level; and her elder brother, of whom she speaks affectionately, is by trade a 'railroad engineer', someone who works with diesel locomotives. As a childhood it can't have been all that easy for either sibling, but one way and another it has stood her in good stead.

———

Q) I still don't understand this cosmic statement of yours. Can you be more specific?

A) I will try and make it clear. I apologise if I repeat myself. Picture yourself as halfway through your first novel. You meet a literary agent at a party, and she (usually a she) asks you, 'And what is your novel about?' You have a glass in your hand, it is a social occasion, she obviously needs a swift reply. What do you say? There's no time for an elaborate narration of the plot – 'There's these two people and he thinks this and she thinks that, and they do this and they do that.' She wants to know how your novel is positioned in the world of human affairs and in particular in that of book marketing: who is going to buy it?

She needs you to tell her what Elizabeth Bowen calls 'the non-poetic statement of a poetic truth'. (Find the reference in her fine essay 'Notes on Writing a Novel', written in 1945 and collected in *The Mulberry Tree*, Vintage, 1999.)

'The poetic truth', the heart of the matter, is the 'cosmic statement'. It is the truth the writer has to arrive at and then describe to the agent at the party, and often finds difficulty doing so. It can seem too simple, almost naïve. But, again quoting my heroine Elizabeth Bowen, it is there to be found

– 'what is left after the whittling away of alternatives', the essential, the 'what is to be said'.

If the agent asked Dickens at a party, 'What's your new novel about, Charles?' he would say, 'Oh, it's about how things can seem the best of times when they're actually the worst of times. It plays out during the French Revolution. I'm calling it *A Tale of Two Cities*.'

Or the agent: 'I hear you're writing a book, E.L. What's it about?' And Ms James will reply: 'Oh, it's about how women love to be dominated. I reckon there's a market out there. I'm calling it *Fifty Shades of Grey* because in this world things are so seldom black or white, good or bad.'

Once you've worked out what your novel is about – it's surprisingly often about your own family situation, though you don't realise it – and faced it, the writing gets surprisingly easier. Okay?

———

Q) What do I do? I have writer's block. I can't write a thing.

A) There's no such thing as writer's block. You may be ill, or not have had breakfast, or be in some emotional turmoil. But most likely – if you haven't just finished and said all you need to say, which is always a possibility to be considered – what you've done is somehow write yourself into a corner. In which case overcome your natural reluctance to read through what you've written, and do so. 'Writer's block', like being 'stuck', doesn't just happen by itself. There is a reason for it. You've somehow lost your way on the path that must lead inexorably through your novel from beginning to end. It can be little – you've made some character say something they wouldn't say in a month of Sundays – or large – your story has taken a turn which will lead you into trouble. Look at it, fix it, and you'll find yourself writing on. Whoever said it would be easy? The act of creation involves getting rid of what you don't want, as a sculptor does with his block of stone.

————

Q) I've written 'The End'. But how can I be sure I've finished?

A) Good question. All your points made and all loose threads tied up; all 'i's dotted, all 't's crossed? The pages are numbered? You've left space on the page for easy editing? Haven't crammed your paragraphs together – you're not trying to save paper; this is an electronic age! (Whenever you've changed time or place it needs to be reflected by space on the page.) Does the text look easy and confident? A crowded page never does, just old-fashioned. Can you stand by every word, argue for every sentence? No careless repetitions, no typos, no relying on some putative editor to sort your problems for you later on? (Editors, publishers, no longer have time or will to do it. You are in a buyers' market.)

Now, take time to look at your first four pages. It's remarkable how often you can simply do without these. You'd written them when you were working yourself in, waffling in sheer terror at the prospect before you – two hundred or more blank pages to be covered – explaining yourself to yourself, temporising, writing and rewriting far too often, anything but actually getting on with the novel. Why it's usually four pages of waffle, not more, not less, I don't know, but this jumping from foot to foot before the race gets going is endemic. Children's books are worst – never judge one by its first four pages.

———

Q) It took me only three months to write my novel. Does this mean it's going to be bad?

A) Not necessarily, any more than a novel which

took seven years to write is bound to be good. Indeed, taking a long time can be a bad thing. The writer will have changed their skin since they began. They will know more, have felt more and with any luck changed their view of the world. The reading world will have changed too. Nothing's static. The beginning of any book is intrinsically linked to its end: the person the writer longed to murder seven years ago may now feel like your dearest friend. The horse you are flogging may not be dead, but it will certainly be rather tired after seven years. Don't take too long about things.

I know people have to work and bring up children, and full-time writing is often not possible – don't lament that too much: peace, quiet and spare time can make you languid and introspective – but do keep your end in sight. I'm afraid the whole thing is much like writing essays at school – the one you worked on so hard and long gets only a C, the one you tossed off when drunk and disorderly gets an

A. There is no justice. But at least having worked so hard for so little apparent reward on one, the next thing you write will come easily. In my experience, one hard-to-write novel is followed by two which flow without effort. So one proceeds.

Hemingway rewrote the end of *A Farewell to Arms* seventeen times – nothing wrong with that – but the whole book was written within the year. Muriel Spark wrote *The Prime of Miss Jean Brodie* in a month. Dostoyevsky wrote *The Gambler* in a week. Just because Flaubert took seven years or so to write *Madame Bovary* it doesn't follow that there is intrinsic merit in a book simply because it took a long time to write.

And don't try and get everything into the first novel you write. With any luck you have a writing life to come. Eke your material out: that was Kingsley Amis's advice to me so I pass it on. A practical man. Eke out all your past excesses. He had plenty.

———

Q) I am inspired by this idea for a novel. It came to me in a dream. Should I follow it through?

A) Inspiration's all very well but it does need to be tempered by reason. Be careful you're not writing a novel which makes sense to no-one but yourself. Dreams are as likely to come from hell as heaven, depending on the state of your unconscious. Of course you must take notice of your unconscious – it probably has more say in the writing of your novel than even you realise – but dreams? They may well be trying to tell *you* something but your reader is not you, and you will need to do a whole lot of dream interpretation and soul searching before passing them on. No matter how vivid and coherent and full of meaning, your dreams are not likely to strike the reader in the same way they do you. Writing is not a magic wand.

The same applies to thoughts you have waking

up in the morning or drifting off to sleep. These can offer an apparently brilliant solution to some hole you wrote yourself into yesterday; on occasion you may indeed have found a way through – but mostly such ideas don't stand up to the glare of morning light. Like dreams, they are creatures of the dark: succubi, leading you on. You can waste an awful lot of time pursuing false leads in this business. Sheer folly can pose as inspiration.

Or perhaps next you'll say: *'I've just had this great "what-if" idea.'* That probably came to you in the night too. Another cause for alarm. What if a dead man walks, what if you wake up as a black beetle, what if you write a novel not using the letter 'e' (a lipogram)? If you're Meyrink or Kafka or Perec the great idea may just about work. But you're probably not a genius, and the trouble with what-if novels is that even though the idea can sound so good and so high-concept that gullible editors commission you – you then have to write the thing, and though the beginning's brilliant what do you do for a middle and an end? It's when writing what-if novels that students find themselves saying *'I've written three chapters and I'm stuck'*, to which the brutal answer from me is usually *'You're not stuck, you're finished.'* It was a short story not a novel. You have said all you have to say.

On occasion all is not lost. There may be some ingenious way through, such as introducing some relevant subplot on the first page, and feeding that in throughout, or realising that the what-if concept was actually the end of the book, not its beginning. It was a really 'so-that's-how-it-turned out!' novel all along. Ingenuity is the novelist's best friend.

———

Q) What age should I make my characters? Does it matter?

A) The answer, alas, matters very much to Marketing

and PR people. You may choose to ignore this horrible fact and pursue your literary ambitions unmoved by the practicalities of publication, but you've asked so you might as well take notice.

It is any writer's first and reasonable instinct to make their main protagonist the same age, roughly, as they are – but consider whether it is a sensible thing to do. Readers come in all sizes, sexes, shapes and ages, but all prefer their novels to feature young women rather than old. This applies particularly, alas, to older women, though they are by far the more prolific readers of fiction. (Men tend to prefer non-fiction – histories, biographies, science, car mechanics.) And older women, my theory is, prefer to identify with themselves when young, not as they are now, in the days when they were a leaping, bounding youngster, sexually active, agile of limb, and not afraid of adventure. It makes for livelier reading.

Publishers, who these days tend to turn away novels by middle-aged women about middle-aged women on the grounds that they are depressing, are probably wise to do so. We now have a sorry state of affairs in which older women, who tend to be the only ones with the time, energy, experience and patience to write novels at all, have an uphill struggle trying to get them published. Whereas a pretty young woman with her face on the back flap sells a lot of books, but has rather less wisdom to pass on than the older woman. What's to be done?

My own answer is always to have a juvenile lead, someone running around in a state of sexual turmoil, while the older woman, keeping a low profile, passes on the wisdom of her more senior years. Get your juvenile lead on the front page: lure the reader in. Twenty-five works better than thirty-five, thirty-five better than forty-five – after fifty, forget it. Theatre plays have been employing such tactics for a long, long time. Women past their nubile prime get fewer parts in films or jobs announcing on TV. It shouldn't be so, and one hopes it's changing, but alas it is so.

Having said all this someone like Roddy Doyle, who writes about women better than anyone I know, will prove me wrong, writing a book which sells like hot cakes about a woman of fifty-five. He got away with Paula being thirty-nine in *The Woman Who Walked Into Doors*, but she *feels* even older to the reader – she's taken to drink; but she wisely spends a long time on the page back as a young woman. And at thirty-nine women haven't given up, as Paula seems to have done. If you're a woman writer you need to bear these fearful things in mind, even if you take no notice. And by the way, do make your protagonist as little like you physically as you can. Otherwise your reader will assume the novel is about the person in the picture on the back flap. It may well be, but try not to let on.

If you're a man you can safely make your male characters any age, while keeping your female characters young and sexy. Try and avoid too great an age gap, though. Readers get queasy if a male hero of pensionable age is loved by a twenty-year-old girl: the writer will quickly find himself under troll attack.

———

Q) Supposing I don't want to write a good novel, I just want to make money?

A) A good question, if seldom put so bluntly. In the popular novel the lowest common denominator rules: that is to say the plot. If you are writing a book and hope to get lots and lots of readers, you will not attempt to follow any instructions from me: rather you will do the opposite. You will eschew cosmic statements in case they lead to unnecessary contemplation and you the writer will keep right out of it. You will use lots and lots of adjectives and you will splash adverbs about

– all the sins for which I chide the aspiring writer. Importantly, you will not use the word 'said' if you can possibly help it. Your characters will screech, whisper, yell, snarl, shout, gasp, yearn, argue, deny, or smile their words, but they will very rarely just say them. If they do, there will an adverb nearby so the reader knows that the words have been said with some strong revealing emotion. He or she will say whatever it is angrily, caressingly, sagely, nastily, kindly, scratchily, benignly, acidly, savagely or despairingly.

Interesting, though, how Lee Child, who is taken seriously as a writer as well as having hordes of readers, manages to avoid 'said' by seldom having more than two people in a room or confined space together, so you don't have to specify which of them is talking. Make of that what you will.

It might be an interesting experiment, for those of you who have had a novel rejected time and time again, to change its title and rewrite, adding two or three extra adjectives to every one you used in the original, and strengthening every verb so your characters don't walk but head for, don't run but hurtle, don't reach for but lunge, don't cry out but scream or yell, don't frown but rage, don't bite but savage, and so on. Change title and names and re-send to a less lofty publisher than you tried first and see what happens. Let me know.

———

Q) You've said very little about dialogue. More, please?

A) I try to have a snatch of dialogue on the first page of a novel. It suggests to the reader that this is a book in which something is going to *happen*; it isn't just going to blether on and on. The very attempt, I find, helps the writer formulate the book so the opening pages are not all back story or description – probably better to avoid – but goes straight into an actual scene, no matter how brief. That said, I do not always manage it myself. I am nevertheless very conscious that large blocks of tightly packed unbroken print at the beginning of a book can put a reader off – especially if the novel comes in e-book form. Space on the page and typography are more and more the writer's business.

Tutors of many creative writing classes will tell you that it is bad form to start a novel with dialogue, but I've done it often enough. It depends what the dialogue is. No good if it's: *'Hello, Betty,' smiled Joan, opening the door to her friend next door. 'Do come in. Can I offer you a cup of tea?'*

'Hello Joan,' chuckled Betty. 'Yes thank you, that's very kind of you.'

If on the other hand you start with: *'Please put the gun down, Betty,' said Joan. 'You can't shoot me because we made a non-aggression pact when we were young. Surely you remember?'*

'A pact's a pact,' said Betty. 'But I'll be doing you a favour. I promised to put you out of your misery if ever you lost your marbles. Now you're marrying this creep it's obvious the time has come...' – you might get away with it.

Cut out the hellos, the goodbyes, anything boring, anything the reader can fill in for themselves. Just as a film editor leaves out the obvious bits, and cuts to mid scene, so the novelist must treat his or her dialogue. Nothing boring or obvious. Cut to the chase. When they're reading dialogue your readers stop watching characters and listen to them instead. Keep it lively. When characters are being active, keep spoken dialogue, direct speech, short and sporadic. When they're reflecting, you can afford to make their sentences longer.

Don't try and replicate real speech, complete with 'um's and 'ah's and 'I mean' – a novel is a written document and speech is formalised to a degree – leave them out. Be sparing with a literal translation of regional accents. One dropped 'g' or missed 'h', one 'ee bah goom' in every twelve is about right. Suggest but don't insist – readers get the gist; don't tire them with detail.

If you ask the question, you're probably dissatisfied with what you're writing. Go through a section of dialogue, and make yourself read it aloud. Put as much of it as you can into reported speech. Cut it to the bone. Make sure the women aren't asking all the questions and the men giving all the answers. (That's arrant old-fashioned sexism.) Make sure you're not using it to further the plot. (Dialogue is for revealing personality.) If the reader isn't told who's speaking, they should be able to work it out from the rhythm of the language and what is being said. (But don't rely on it: tell them!) It should be better now.

———

Q) Please, more about that cosmic statement?

A) Okay. I know it's tricky. Perhaps some more examples would help? The ultimate cutting exercise – the novel in a sentence, before it's even written. (The synopsis is bad enough. In a perfect world one would write the novel before the synopsis, anyway. I once lost a publisher because the novel I submitted had nothing to do with the synopsis and they'd already done the jacket drawing. They were ever so cross. So was I. The world is not perfect.)

By a 'cosmic statement' I mean a sentence that sums up some universal truth, and applies to what you mean to write about. It also suggests the presence, otherwise unspoken, of an all-knowing writer whom the reader can safely trust to be interesting and thoughtful. It can be light and ironic or sombre and philosophical. It will set the tone and ensure you keep to the point for the whole book, so your last few pages are not so very different from the first.

Some writers manage to get the elusive sentence

into their first line, and can then spend the next 80,000 words happily developing the theme, going back at moments of doubt – which always come – to that first sentence to be reminded of what their novel is *about* in the first place.

Take as examples these famous beginnings, cosmic sentences, statements of the writer's intent.

'Happy families are all alike; every unhappy family is unhappy in its own way.'

Leo Tolstoy, *Anna Karenina*

'All this happened, more or less.'

Kurt Vonnegut, *Slaughterhouse Five*

'Lolita, light of my life, fire of my loins. My sin, my soul.'

Vladimir Nabokov, *Lolita*

And then proceed to write on, as this lot did. But

these particular hints are for writers of literary novels: those in which the writer's ambition is more than just to make money, not just to entertain but to offer up an opinion as to the nature of the universe and the people in it. You can get to it young – Jane Austen wrote her *Pride and Prejudice* first line when she was twenty-two, an age when she wouldn't have had much experience of life, but at least she knew her own family. Tolstoy wrote *Anna Karenina*'s opening when he was fifty and had form in wretched marriages (I think he was wrong about them, but never mind). All of the first lines listed above come from what I would call opinionated writers. I would not call Dan Brown an opinionated writer, just a very, very successful one.

'Renowned curator Jacques Saunière staggered through the vaulted archway of the museum's Grand Gallery,' is the *Da Vinci Code*'s opening sentence, thus breaking every possible rule, but he does cut to the chase, getting into fourteen words what many another writer would take as many sentences to achieve.

———

Q) I'm lost for a subject. Please help?

A) If you know you want to write a novel and still have no knowledge of what you want to write it about – it can happen – you could do worse than look up Latin tags on the internet. Latin tags – usually phrases written by ancient Romans, and used by well-educated generations of Europeans for centuries since – were known to contain the concentrated wisdom of the ages, and they are more than likely to still apply to us today. Great civilisations rise and fall; human nature does not change. A Latin tag can be a good way of getting to your cosmic statement, on which you are to base the entirety of your novel. Here are a few examples:

Exitus probat acta – 'The end justifies the means.'
A mystery, perhaps, about a jealous elder sister
who sleeps with her brother-in-law out of
malice, only to discover the younger sister is
even wickeder than she is. Title: *A Justified Girl*,
bearing in mind how popular titles with 'girl' in
them currently are on Amazon.

Video et taceo – Elizabeth I's motto: 'I see but stay
silent.' A CIA thriller perhaps, the fate of the
man who sees too much. Title: *The Witness*.

Ovid's *Video meliora proboque deteriora sequor* –
'I see the better way, but I follow the worse.'
An inveterate gambler marries an alcoholic –
a moral tale. Title: *My Life in a Country and
Western Song*.

Eheu fugaces labuntur anni – 'Alas, the fleeting years
slip away.' Title: *Remembrance of Things Past*.

Fallaces sunt rerum species – 'Appearances are deceptive.' People pretend to be what they are not. Title: *Gone Girl*.

Fiat justitia ruat coelum – 'Let justice be done though the heavens fall.' A paranoiac detective follows a charming criminal. Title: *Let's Get Out of Here*.

Other sentiments that might inspire you, cosmic statements all:

Legum servi sumus ut liberi esse possimus – 'We are slaves of the law so we can be free.'

Omnia mutantur, nos et mutamur in illis – 'All things change, and we change with them.'

Pessimum genus inimicorum laudantes – 'Flatterers are the worst type of enemy.'

Proprium humani ingenii est odisse quem laeseris –
'It is human nature to hate a person whom
you have injured.'

Radix omnium malorum est cupiditas –
'The love of money is the root of all evil.'

Struit insidias lacrimis cum femina plorat –
'When a woman weeps, you can be
sure she is plotting.'

And so forth and so on. If all else fails, go to your
local newspaper, find a story which fascinates you,
attach a Latin tag, and see how the story can be first
universalised, then novelised. Hardy worked from
press cuttings for *Tess of the d'Urbervilles*, Flaubert
for *Madame Bovary*; don't be sniffy.

———

Q) How do you yourself set about writing a novel?

A) The beginning of a pure, non-meta novel is always the most difficult, a once a year event for me. The first three months is spent in guilty idleness, the next three months with a lot of unconscious rumblings, three months or so of speculation and no actual writing, then panic and necessity set in and I write the title first (which, like the cosmic statement, I will have decided upon at some time in the last six months) and then the novel itself.

'What's your next book about?' someone will have asked me, and I will have had to answer, or 'What's it called?' and I have time to work it out, though often, like naming characters, it comes on the instant.

I have learned to write my own first page six, seven or more times, changing tenses, voices and mood each time until I arrive at the version in which all the ingredients seem to meld together properly and the novel seems simple and obvious and something I look forward to writing. I will have come to various decisions over the last months (well, put it more truthfully, they have been flickering and flittering through my mind for ages, but if it helps you, use this as a check list):

* How am I best going to deliver this story, make my point, persuade others to my point of view?
* Do I know more or less what and who I am writing about?
* Would this work best as a Dear Reader novel (in which I as the writer show my presence, talk to the reader conversationally, seemingly taking them into my confidence), and if it would, to what extent will the 'I' be fictional or my real self?
* Do I have the stamina, and does the story have enough depth, to sustain a third-person omniscient narrator – who has to make moral judgements? Or should I keep out of it and just tell the story out of a character's head? Or more

than one head to make it easier? How many heads can I get away with?

* Out of whose eyes, and how many, do I intend to look?

* Is enough going to be happening to get away with the present tense: or perhaps anyway I need the objectivity which comes with third-person past tense.

* How do I envisage my reader: looking at an e-book or turning pages?

* Am I taking this lightly or dead seriously?

* Do I know more or less how it is going to end, because the end must be closely linked with the beginning?

Only when I have briefed myself properly on what and how I intend to write will I carry on – referring to my first page from time to time to reassure myself I am still on track. It will be my bible. I may tell myself and others I make it up as I go along, and

have the sensation that the novel unfolds before me –
but most of the work, I realise, consists in getting the
first page right. And it can take a couple of days of
conscious thought or a few months of unconscious
brooding. Make it up as you go along, but know
what you are doing before you begin.

I tell you this story as a warning. Once, back in
the eighties, I had a brilliant what-if idea. It was
about cloning and its reverse: one shared personality spread out between too many bodies, or too
many personalities crammed into one body. I had
'flu at the time, but not, alas, badly enough to stop
me covering sheets of paper with words – in those
days handwritten. I posted off the idea in four
different directions – novel, stage, TV and radio.
All were commissioned. It was four whole years
by the time I'd worked through to the end of all of
them. All those middles waiting to be found, all
those conclusions waiting to be reached, ingenuity
stretched to its furthest limits. Aarrgghh…

Part Five

A life in writing

I'd written some twenty-five novels before I went anywhere near a creative writing class, and then I went as a tutor not a student. So I missed out on the conventional terminology – I still have to look up terms like 'unreliable narrator' and 'foreshadowing' on Wikipedia to understand exactly what they mean. Most turn out to be tools novelists have been using forever anyway, without knowing the jargon.

There is an endless source of information out there on the web, much of it very useful, but some of it rather odd. When it comes to fictional 'character', it is supposed to matter very much that the reader should 'care' about the protagonists. This often gets misconstrued by today's novelists, so many of whom go to creative writing classes: they assume that they ought to make their characters nice. People can be likeable without being nice.

I care about real living people for all kinds of reasons. I care about some people that some other people think are perfectly horrid. You don't make best friends at school with the nicest, best-behaved girl in the class – she's usually a bit boring. You make friends with someone who makes you laugh, or sparks up your own ideas, who knows where you're coming from, with whom you have something in common. Why should readers be any different? Everyone remembers Becky Sharp in *Vanity Fair* – she's spiteful and dangerous: people tend to forget Amelia, who is so nice and good.

Don't keep your protagonists reactive, keep them

active. Give them faults, the kind your readers can identify with. Give them terrible troubles, by all means – so we can see how they face up to them. Above all, make things *happen*. Don't take up a whole novel making your protagonist learn a lesson, be a nicer person. Keep your characters as non-PC as you can manage without being trolled. Is *Pride and Prejudice* a novel about how wrong Elizabeth was to judge a suitor on first impressions, or more about how she snaffled the best man in town by being impertinent? No. It's about pride and prejudice, and how luckily for Elizabeth it worked out.

If you look on Google you will find sites telling you to make a character profile of your protagonists before you begin writing: thus you will 'know your character'. It's not how I would ever set about it: it's the kind of thing TV script editors insist on – but that is so that more than one writer can work on a running script, and thus keep the stories consistent throughout a series. I wouldn't have thought writing a profile for a character in a novel was at all advisable. In a lifetime of novel writing I have never done such a thing. (Which isn't to say the novels mightn't have been better if I had – just that it never occurred to me, any more than would writing profiles of friends or family. The complexity of it would defeat me.) All novelists go about things differently. There is no one way of doing anything.

But my training – and I did have a training, and a rigorous one – though not in a creative writing class but in an advertising agency – led me to set about things differently. By the time I started writing novels I had had more than enough experience in the creation of character, even in thirty-second bites or a half-page spread in the daily newspaper.

I started out in advertising as a copywriter. Most ads in those days were little stories told in a few lines, and a big illustration above, selling a product. The characters would be stereotypes – there was no space for anything else – happy housewife, anxious girl, angry husband, man with headache, wise doctor, foolish friend. The art director needed two or three words of description to do the illustration, no more. When I branched out into writing TV commercials, there'd be a casting director. You'd ask them to find a pretty girl with long legs, or a loving young mother with a cute baby – still only a few words of description, but still the stereotype – and the commercial was fifteen or thirty seconds long. If you were very lucky you'd have sixty seconds in which to tell your story and sell your product.

Moving on to the more fertile ground of stage plays and TV dramas, in which one was selling ideas, not product, I had a few more lines in which to branch away from the stereotype, and offer everyone involved a guide to what the writer had in mind. A stage play or screenplay is a blueprint from which everyone involved in this group activity has to work – lighting man, producer, props, director, actor – so you keep instructions as brief and telling as possible. I realised soon that what you needed to describe was how a character deviated from the norm. The casting director's nature was to cast everyone middle: middle height, middle class, middle looks, even temperament unless you mentioned otherwise. If you wrote 'tall' or 'short' or 'wall-eyed' or 'bow-legged' or 'bad-tempered' they would oblige you: otherwise it was just middle. And that is what I find I do in a novel: if characters have normal eyes you don't mention them, if they are startlingly blue you do. If they have a wooden leg you mention it, or if they have been married five times not the normal one or two you mention that. Otherwise your reader, like your casting director, casts 'middle' in his or her head, and just gets on with it.

My early novels were novelisations of my TV plays – I had the plot, structure, the lines all worked out, I'd left it to the actors to develop character, and some very good actors at that. I suspect I use characters to work out my own ideas about what life is like. They represent different trends in contemporary society. They tend towards the stereotypical, I admit. But it's deliberate because this is part of a fictional character's appeal: the part the reader recognises immediately, identifies with: the aspect the reader responds to, and so worries with them about how they'll get out of the situation into which I've cast them. Your character doesn't have to be nice and good to be empathised with: he or she has to be recognised as an identifiable, noticeable individual, with certain personality traits.

I see the novels I write as fictionalised essays used to prove a point I want to make. I am by nature a didactic novelist, while joking away to hide it as best I can, if only so as not to frighten the reader. My characters exist to carry through a plot; I'm not bothering all that much whether they're 'rounded' or not. I give them quirks and fads and foibles as they occur to me, but I never let them run away with the story. They are mine and they do as I tell them.

If I examine my protagonists I can see they tend to be one quarter stereotype – as in those early advertisements – for rapid identification and recognition; one quarter myself – I am the one doing the writing after all, and autobiography can never be far away; the third quarter a mélange of all the people I've ever known; and the final quarter is sheer invention – where I take the most liberties, have the most fun, summon up someone from the depths of the group unconscious who had no reality before. The character grows as the story grows. He or she can hardly be 'profiled' in advance.

I like to know all kinds of trivia about my characters, what they put in their fridge; whether they prefer showers to baths; how they get on with their grannies; the conversation between their parents when they were born and how they came to have the names I've given them. These things

I write as I discover them, as I look inside their fridges, overhear their conversations – not before they begin: I am the fly on their walls. As well they're not real.

I know the situation my character is going into rather than exactly who the character is. Then she – it is usually a she – emerges. She starts off as a stereotype. Little by little features and characteristics emerge. I look into her knicker drawer and find out about her sex life. I feel I am as much friendly spy as creator.

I started out by novelising my own TV dramas, setting clearly delineated scenes, starting the action mid scene, using the actors to flesh out the characters, moving the action on in every scene as I did on TV, and getting out and on fast, never letting anyone say hello or goodbye. I trained as an economist, never studied literature; 'creative writing' had not been invented. I had only first principles to work with. I could see the limitations of what I was doing and how I was doing it and branched out as the novel allows one to more easily than TV, into experiments with structure, time, form and theme, and have continued to do so.

Different stories require different structures: in some novels I am an omniscient narrator, in some an unreliable one. Some, which require little reflection and more action, I write in the present tense and first person, some in the past tense and third person. Occasionally I write metafiction, a kind of ironic alienation device in which one draws attention to the fact that what is being read is only fiction.

I did this in 1983, in a book called *Letters to Alice*, a half-fact, half-epistolary novel. It started out as a coffee table book about Jane Austen, on whose life I was meant to be an expert – I was not – having recently adapted *Pride and Prejudice* for TV (still there on You Tube: the 1982 version). I said yes and did my best. But I had written very little non-fiction before then – all that cutting and pasting, restructuring, editing and re-editing, to get an argument straight and convincing, while if you make everything up it just flows and is easy to write. So I introduced as much fiction as I could, inventing a fictional niece (Alice), and writing her letters, as myself in the first person, about the craft of fiction. It is, thankfully, still in print, though initially the publishers were dismayed. They'd rather expected a picture book with captions.

I have written a great deal in my lifetime: indeed I have become a writeaholic. As the alcoholic reaches for his bottle on waking, I stagger to the office and write. When I was an all-purpose writer and young, I wrote commercials, radio dramas, plays, stage plays, TV and film scripts, musicals, documentaries, reviews, forewords, speeches, novels – anything for anyone who asked – but have now settled down to writing mostly novels.

It seemed to me that when one wrote in a different media to a different audience it was as if you were slotting a different program into your computer. Once you had learned how to do one book review, for example – looked up a few to see how they were done and absorbed the pattern – one could then simply go into review mode whenever required. And the same for all the other media. It has been a learning curve that hasn't stopped. I was a reading child but not a writing child. I never kept a diary, struggled with thank-you letters, wrote only two stories in my schooldays – one in 1942 when I was eleven in New Zealand, one in 1946 in London when I was fifteen, and only wrote those because I had to. I remember every detail of them but found myself quite shocked by the kind of ultrareality you could achieve with words: it was far too strong for me, and too like hard work any-way. I loved English grammar but the study of Eng. Lit. baffled me. They kept asking what the writer meant by this and that, and all I could say was 'why, what they said', which never pleased anyone. But I learned how to disguise my ignorance in exams by manipulating words.

At university I honed this skill, studying Economics and learning how to simplify jargon and how doing so would get you good marks.

After university I worked for a year as a temporary assistant clerk at the Foreign Office where I learned the arts of propaganda and how to create fake news, in a department where spies, romantic men in fedora hats, passed by the office door.

Then I became an unmarried mother and for five years learned if not how to write better at least a great deal about the human condition, so that when I started writing novels, which didn't happen until I was thirty-five, at least I found I had 'something to say'. They were not wasted years, though not very pleasant.

Then in the sixties I became an advertising copywriter in a top *Mad Men* office, and learned the arts of persuasion: how to sell: the importance of typography, the difference the order of words can make, how to be economical with the truth, how always to respect your audience and understand the differences between socio-economic groups (a) to (e), and how to survive continual rejection. Copy sent back and back until finally you got it right. It was a wonderful training. When I submitted my first novel in 1966 it was accepted without demur. I thought that was because I was a wonderful writer. But it wasn't. It was because I had learned how to have nothing turned down.

Then I became a TV dramatist. In a TV commercial you sell product: in a TV drama you can sell ideas, but using the same techniques. There I learned to write dialogue actors can speak, how to construct a story and how to cut out all irrelevancies. Moving cameras about is expensive. It was a time when the writer was king; script editors did not exist (TV drama was in its infancy and all but live – in 1969 I was allowed one expensive cut per thirty minutes of screen time. Ingenuity was required.) In those exciting times it took only six weeks between conception and screening. Now it can be five years.

As a radio writer I learned to appeal to an audience through their ears only. As a stage playwright I found how audiences pay attention when a man and a young woman are on stage but fall asleep if two women are talking. Terrible lessons.

And by that time I was indeed a writeaholic, and felt that I had learned quite enough anyway.

But then I started teaching – the more you teach the more you learn – and I had to rethink all over again. Thank you all those who have helped me write this book – by being in class and asking questions.

Finale

I daresay the writing gene will continue on its rambling path through the generations. My grandfather, my mother, my father, my uncle, all wrote novels of varying quality and degrees of success. There always has to be someone around to create this stockpile of alternative universes. Who knows what will happen next, when they'll be needed? See me as the old shambling caretaker down at the recycling centre. Do this, do that. Put this here, put that there, don't do that on any account, more than my job's worth etc. Somebody has to do it.

The writer, like the criminal, has always been at the base of an inverted pyramid, providing work and profit for others. The greatest good, politicians have observed, lies in the providing of employment.

The criminal's one delinquent act provides work and wages for policemen and women, prison warders, court officials, solicitors, barristers, judges, journalists, academics, criminologists, legislators. Similarly, the writer's act of creation – making something where there was nothing there before – provides work for agents, publishers, copy editors, designers, printers, typographers, booksellers, sales reps, publicists, teachers, professors, critics, reviewers, journalists, librarians, festival organisers, academics, historians, cultural commentators and commissars of all kinds. That's a whole lot of people. Let them be grateful to you, not the other way round!

Further reading

On Writing – Stephen King

Aspects of the Novel – E. M. Forster

Bagombo Snuff Box: Uncollected Short Fiction – Kurt Vonnegut (Introduction)

Palm Sunday – Kurt Vonnegut (fourth chapter: 'Triage')

Poetics – Aristotle

How to Write Like Tolstoy: A Journey into the Minds of Our Greatest Writers – Richard Cohen

10 Rules of Writing – Elmore Leonard

A Novel in a Year: A Novelist's Guide to Being a Novelist – Louise Doughty

Why Do I Write? An Exchange of Views between Elizabeth Bowen, Graham Greene and V. S. Pritchett